Martin Wittmann * Infographics: no.parking

Zusammenarbeit mit / In collaboration with: Franziska Maria Hack & Hermann Gummerer

TOTAL ALLES ÜBER BAYERN

THE COMPLETE BAVARIA

Folio

Du blau? Ich weiß!
It's all here in blue and white!

Die berühmten Farben bayerischer Institutionen, in einheitliche Formen gegossen / The famous colours of the Bavarian institutions, cast from a single mould

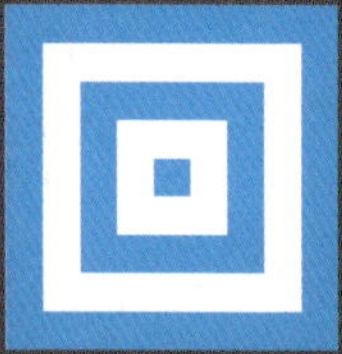

Landesfarben
State colours

Wappen von München
Coat of arms of Munich

Münchner U-Bahn-Netz
Munich underground network

Bayerische Staatliche Polizei
Bavarian State Police

Bayerisches Wappen
Coat of arms of Bavaria

Siemens

ADAC

BMW

Audi

Augustiner-Bräu, Etikett
Augustiner Beer, label

Jim Knopf
(Augsburger Puppenkiste)
(Augsburger puppet show)

CSU-Alleinregierung seit 1962 (Ausnahme: CSU-FDP-Koalition 2008–2013) / CSU one-party government since 1962 (exception: CSU-FDP coalition 2008–2013)

LaBrassBanda
Album „Europa“

Leberkäse
Meat loaf

Nürnberger
Rostbratwürste „Drei im Weggla“
Nuremberg roast bratwurst
“Three on a roll“

24 Stunden
24 hours

Was sich so alles im Lauf eines Tages in Bayern ereignet /
All that happens on an average day in Bavaria

293
Kinder kommen auf die Welt (151 Buben und 142 Mädchen).
children are born (151 boys and 142 girls).

163
Ehen werden geschlossen.
weddings take place.

5.463.835,62 €
Kirchensteuer wird eingenommen.
in church taxes is collected.

68
Ehen werden geschieden.
divorces are finalised.

286.696
Personen fahren mit einer Seilbahn.
people ride on an aerial tramway.

3.479.901
Personen fahren mit dem Liniennahverkehr.
people take local public transport.

590
Führerscheine werden ausgestellt.
driver's licences are issued.

178 g
Lebensmittel schme der Bayer täglich w
is the amount of foo the average Bavaria throws away every d

361
Gewerbe werden angemeldet.
businesses are registered.

9
Unternehmen melden Insolvenz an. companies apply for insolvency.

403.561.644 €
Wert der Waren, die importiert werden
Value of goods imported

454.246.575 €
Wert der Waren, die exportiert werd
Value of goods expor

116.781
Personen fliegen mit dem Flugzeug.
people fly in a plane.

129 l
Wasserverbrauch pro Kopf und Tag
Daily per capita water consumption

116.222 MWh
Atomstrom werden produziert.
of nuclear power are produced.

31.190 MWh
Strom aus erneuerbaren Energien werden produziert.
of power is produced from renewable energies.

19
Personen werden eingebürgert.
people are naturalised.

88.937
Touristen kommen an.
tourists arrive.

77
Wohngebäude werden fertiggestellt.
residential buildings are completed.

68.219 hl
Bier werden gebraut.
of beer is brewed.

6.590.000
Personen arbeiten.
people work.

1.004
Personen ziehen nach Bayern zu.
people move to Bavaria.

736
Personen ziehen aus Bayern fort.
people move away from Bavaria.

48.282,5 hl
Abwasser werden entsorgt.
of wastewater is disposed of.

21.682 t
Milch werden erzeugt.
of milk are produced.

3.342.466
Eier werden gelegt.
eggs are laid.

14.540
Schweine werden geschlachtet.
pigs are slaughtered.

344
Personen sterben.
people die.

Wir sind das Volk

We are the people

Zahlen, bitte: So viele Bayern gibt es / Numbers, please: How many Bavarians are there?

Muss i denn zum Städtele hinein:
Landflucht in Bayern / The rural exodus in Bavaria

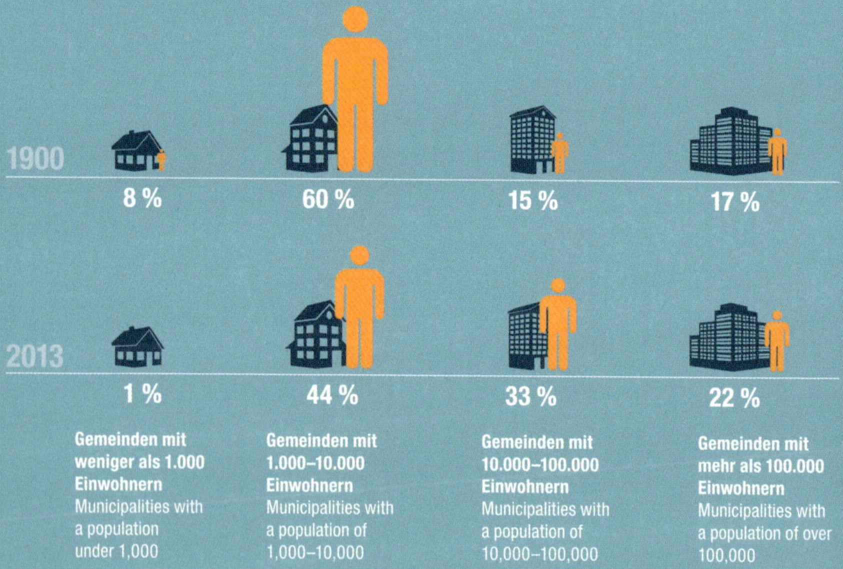

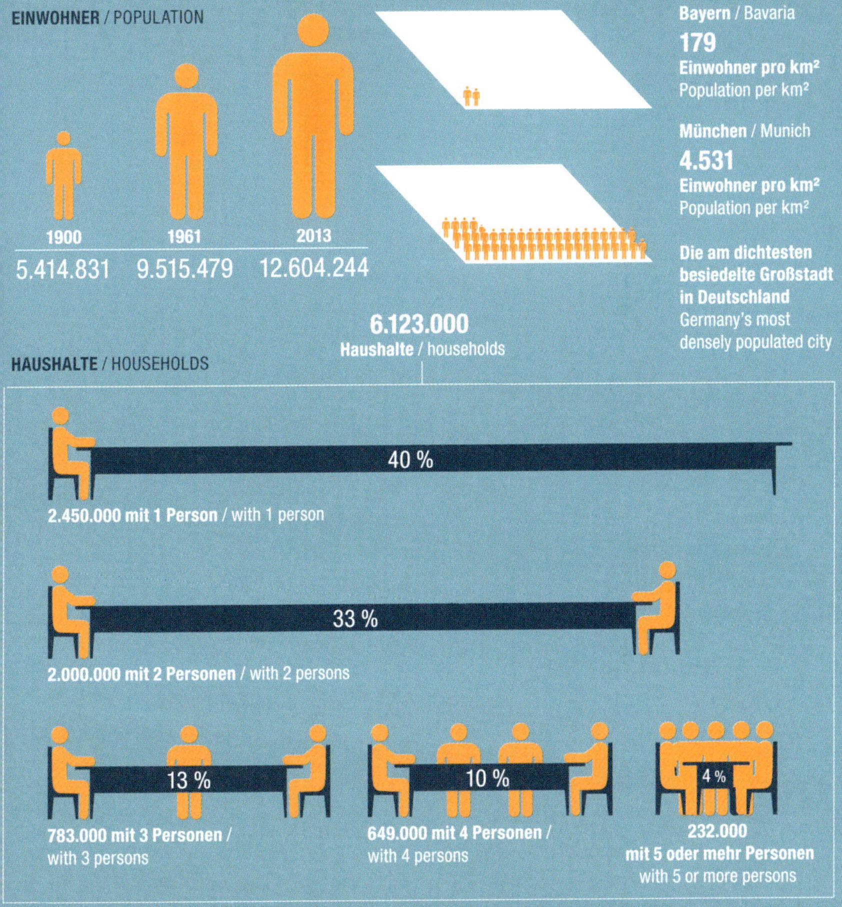
EINWOHNER / POPULATION
1900
5.414.831
1961
9.515.479
2013
12.604.244
Bayern / Bavaria
179
Einwohner pro km²
Population per km²
München / Munich
4.531
Einwohner pro km²
Population per km²
Die am dichtesten besiedelte Großstadt in Deutschland
Germany's most densely populated city
6.123.000
Haushalte / households
HAUSHALTE / HOUSEHOLDS
40 %
2.450.000 mit 1 Person / with 1 person
33 %
2.000.000 mit 2 Personen / with 2 persons
13 %
783.000 mit 3 Personen / with 3 persons
10 %
649.000 mit 4 Personen / with 4 persons
4 %
232.000
mit 5 oder mehr Personen
with 5 or more persons

Die Welt zu Gast bei Freunden
A time to make friends

Na, servus: Wo Bayerns Ausländer herkommen – und wo bayerische Auswanderer hingehen / Na, servus: Where foreigners in Bavaria come from – and where Bavarian émigrés relocate

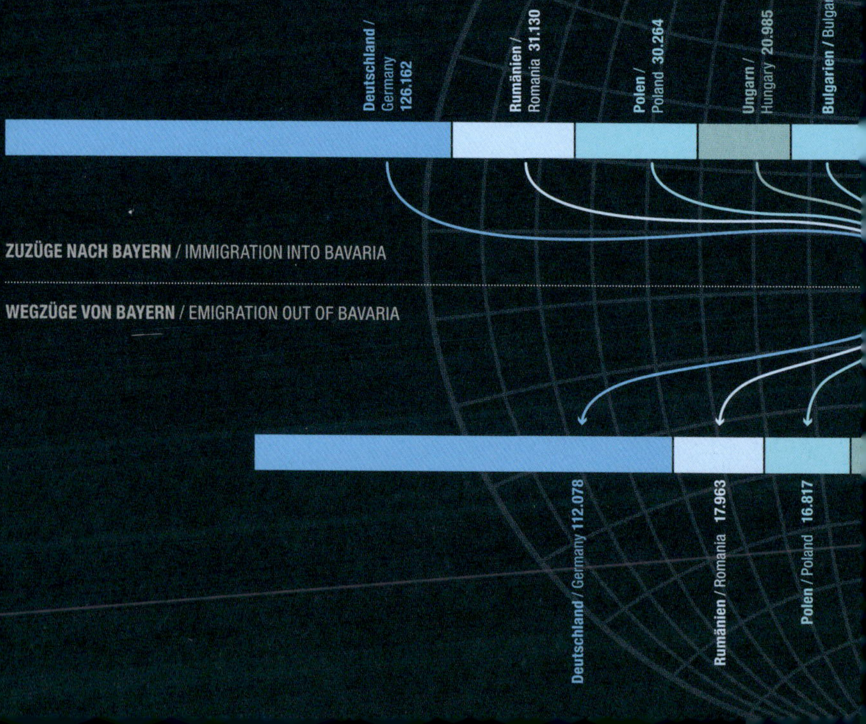

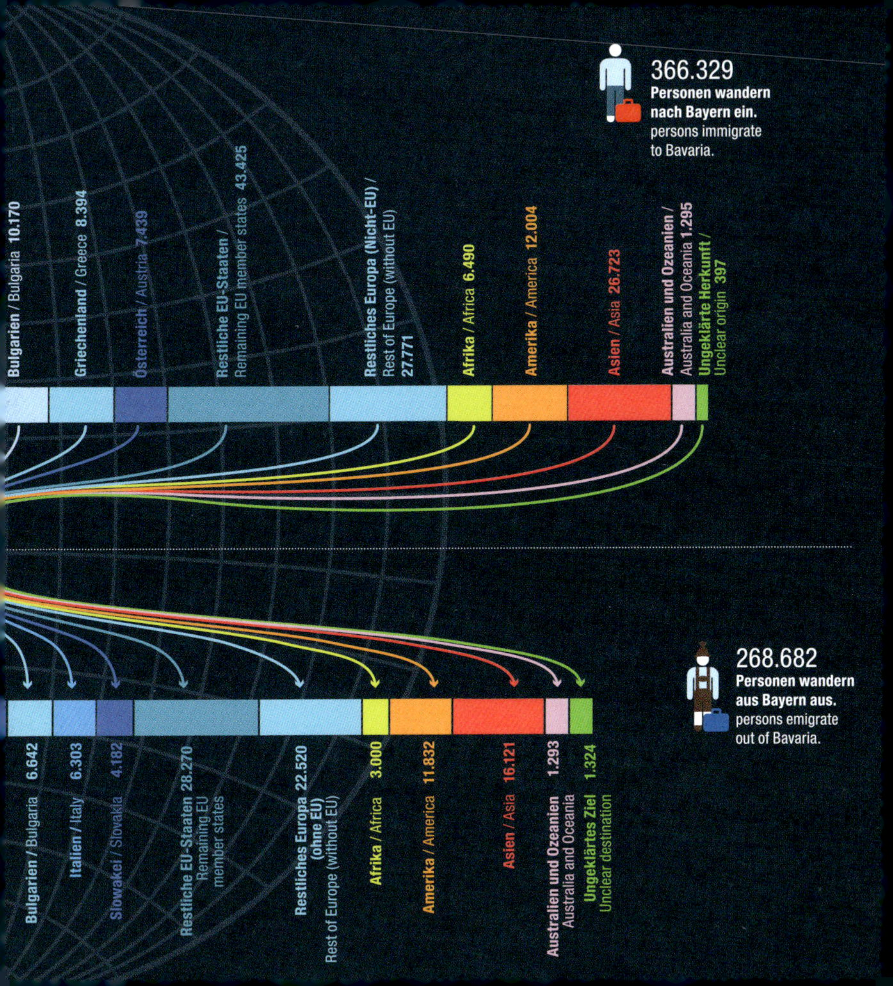
366.329
Personen wandern nach Bayern ein.
persons immigrate to Bavaria.
Bulgarien / Bulgaria 10.170
Griechenland / Greece 8.394
Österreich / Austria 7.439
Restliche EU-Staaten / Remaining EU member states 43.425
Restliches Europa (Nicht-EU) / Rest of Europe (without EU) 27.771
Afrika / Africa 6.490
Amerika / America 12.004
Asien / Asia 26.723
Australien und Ozeanien / Australia and Oceania 1.295
Ungeklärte Herkunft / Unclear origin 397
268.682
Personen wandern aus Bayern aus.
persons emigrate out of Bavaria.
Bulgarien / Bulgaria 6.642
Italien / Italy 6.303
Slowakei / Slovakia 4.182
Restliche EU-Staaten Remaining EU member states 28.270
Restliches Europa (ohne EU) Rest of Europe (without EU) 22.520
Afrika / Africa 3.000
Amerika / America 11.832
Asien / Asia 16.121
Australien und Ozeanien Australia and Oceania 1.293
Ungeklärtes Ziel Unclear destination 1.324

Mia san mia

We are what we are

Die beliebtesten Vornamen und gängigsten Nachnamen der Bayern / Bavaria's most popular first names and most common surnames

Die geografische Verbreitung der typischen Familiennamen Bayerns

The geographical distribution of typical Bavarian family names

Insel der Narrischen

Island of fools

Ja, wo samma denn? Wer denkt sich solche Ortsnamen aus? Und das in Bayern. Und außerhalb sowieso. / Where are we anyway? Who thinks up town names like these? And in Bavaria of all places. Just like everywhere else in the world.

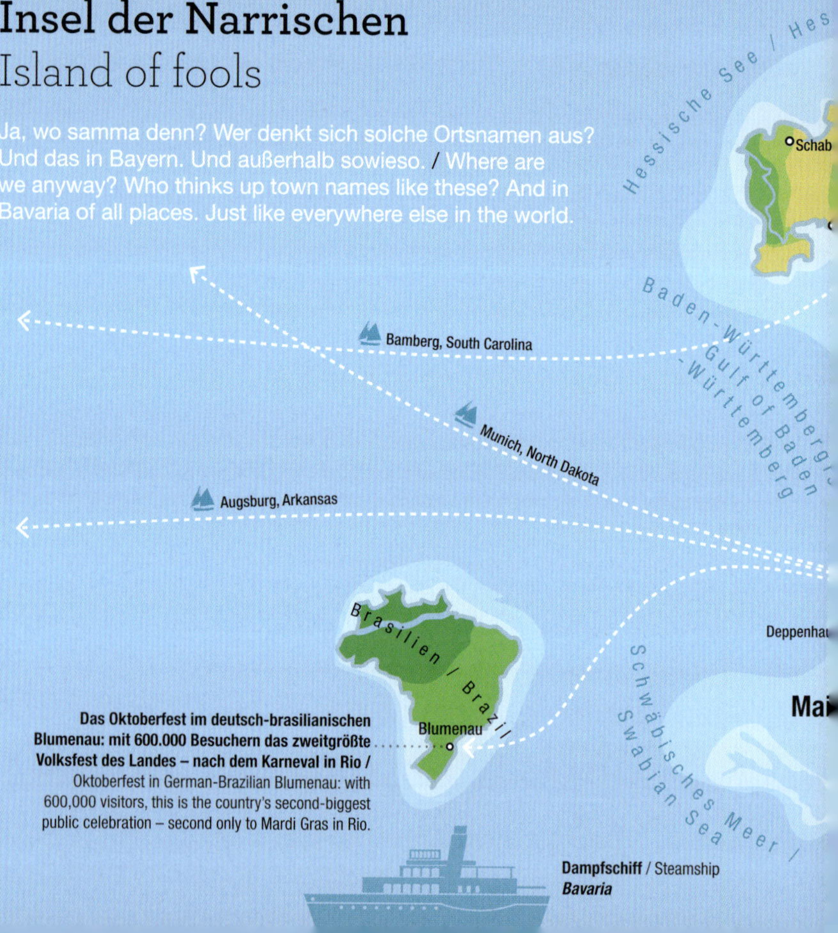

Das Internationale Samba-Festival in Coburg lockt jährlich rund 200.000 Besucher an und ist damit das größte Samba-Festival außerhalb Brasiliens. / The International Samba Festival in Coburg lures some 200,000 visitors and is thus the biggest samba festival outside Brazil.

Otto Normalbayer

Just your average Bavarian

Was zeichnet einen durchschnittlichen Bayern aus? / What makes a Bavarian?

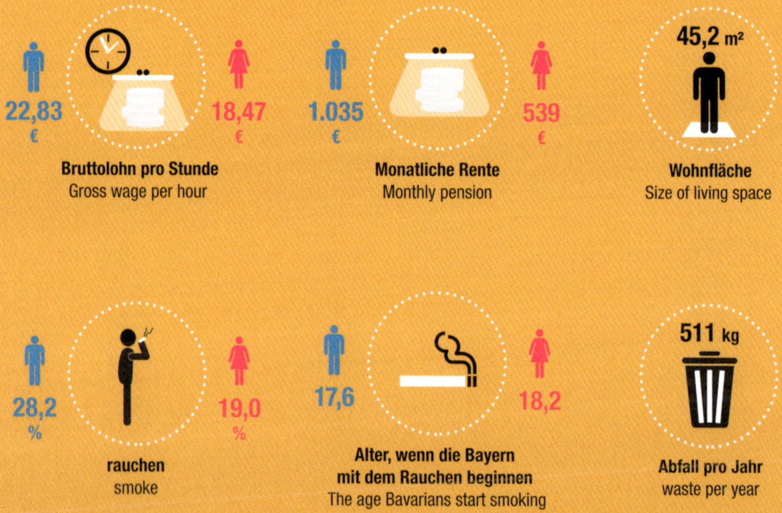

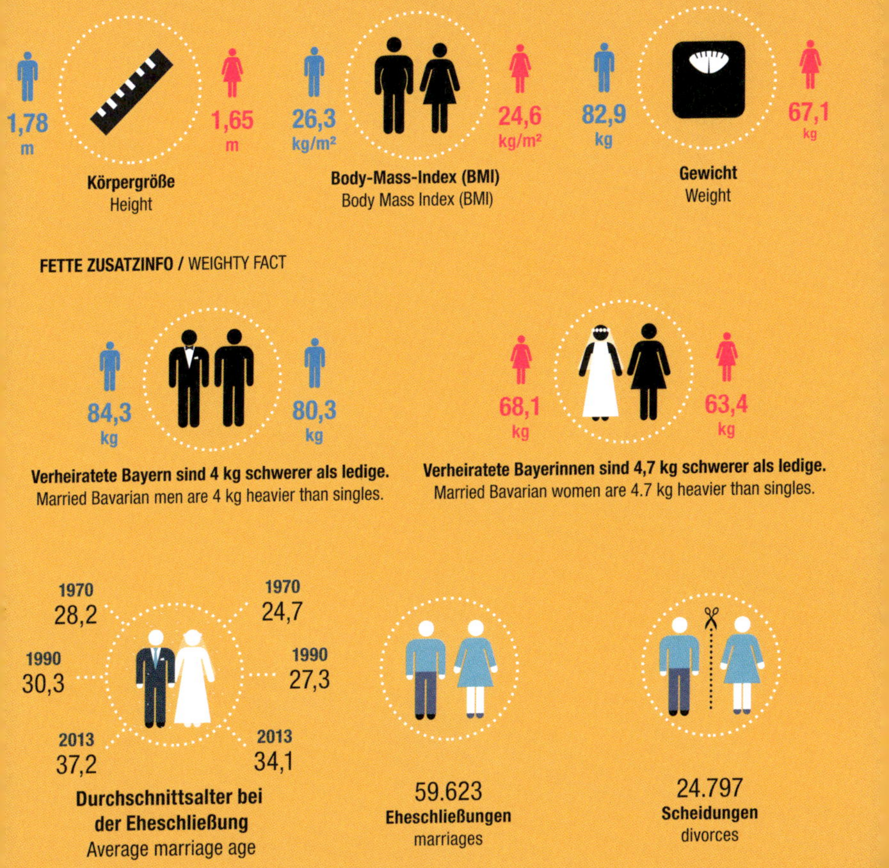
1,78 m
Körpergröße
Height
1,65 m
26,3 kg/m²
Body-Mass-Index (BMI)
Body Mass Index (BMI)
24,6 kg/m²
82,9 kg
Gewicht
Weight
67,1 kg
FETTE ZUSATZINFO / WEIGHTY FACT
84,3 kg
80,3 kg
Verheiratete Bayern sind 4 kg schwerer als ledige.
Married Bavarian men are 4 kg heavier than singles.
68,1 kg
63,4 kg
Verheiratete Bayerinnen sind 4,7 kg schwerer als ledige.
Married Bavarian women are 4.7 kg heavier than singles.
1970
28,2
1990
30,3
2013
37,2
1970
24,7
1990
27,3
2013
34,1
Durchschnittsalter bei der Eheschließung
Average marriage age
59.623
Eheschließungen
marriages
24.797
Scheidungen
divorces

Was machen die bloß?
What on earth do they do?

Heilende Hände, schlimme Finger, grüne Daumen – die Berufe und Berufungen der Bayern. Eine qualifizierte Auswahl. / Healing hands, sneaky fingers, green thumbs – the occupations and vocations of the Bavarians. A qualified selection.

6.590.000
Erwerbstätige
employed

264.523
Arbeitslose
unemployed

25.321
selbstständige Ärzte (in freier Praxis)
self-employed physicians (in private practice)

1.120
Kinderärzte
paediatricians

941
Augenärzte
ophthalmologists

10.990
Zahnärzte (in freier Praxis)
dentists (in private practice)

24.646
Krankenhausärzte
hospital physicians

64.412
Pflegepersonal im Krankenhaus
hospital nursing sta

94.501
Mitarbeiter in Pflegeheimen
nursing home staff

14.254
Apotheker
dispensing chemists

1
Boandlkramer
Grim Reaper

1.480.411
Schüler
pupils

355.915
Studierende
university students

92.244
Lehrer
teachers

241.600
Arbeitskräfte in der Landwirtschaft
agricultural workers

23
Fußball-WM-Teilnehmer (2014) aus bayerischen Vereinen
World Cup football participants (2014) from Bavarian clubs

53
Mörder
killers

1.282
Straßenbahnführer
tram drivers

16.622
Busfahrer
bus drivers

1
Drei-Sterne-Koch
three-star chef

46.000
Jäger
hunters

4.613
Katholische Priester
Catholic priests

3.878
Evangelische Pfarrer
Protestant pastors
davon weiblich
thereof female
721

4
Tatort-Hauptkommissare
chief inspectors on the TV series "Tatort"

467
Menschlein tummeln sich im Wimmelbuch München.
little people are concealed in the Munich hidden object book.

122.626
Straftäter
criminal offenders

Dialektik des Freistaats
Bavarian dialectics

n Bayern wird nicht einfach nur ein Dialekt gesprochen, sondern viele bairische, änkische und alemannische Mundarten. Eine Gemeinsamkeit aber haben sie alle: uswärtige verstehen kaum ein Wort. Zwei Beispiele / Instead of a single dialect, variety of Bavarian, Franconian and Alemmanic vernaculars are spoken in the state. ut they all have one thing in common: outsiders can hardly understand a word. wo examples:

Mädchen / Girl

Bayerische Gebärden
Bavarian signs

Wie Gehörlose bayerische Begriffe gebärden – und warum die im Süden manchmal anders aussehen als im Norden / How the deaf sign typical Bavarian terms – and why they sometimes look different in the south than in the north

SONNTAG / SUNDAY

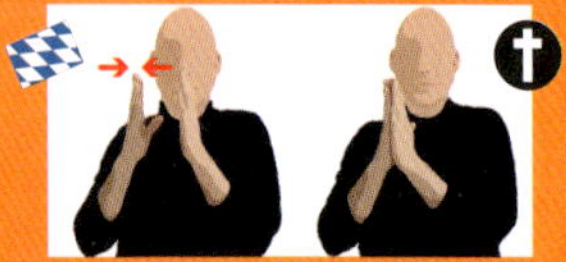

Im Süden ist der Sonntag mit einem Kirchgang verbunden, im Norden mit feiner Kleidung.
In the south, Sunday is associated with going to church and in the north, with dressing up.

WEISSWURST
WHITE SAUSAGE

In Bayern haben sich die Metzger früher die Wurstketten über die Schulter geworfen.
The Bavarian butchers used to throw the sausage links over their shoulder.

RETTICH / RADISH

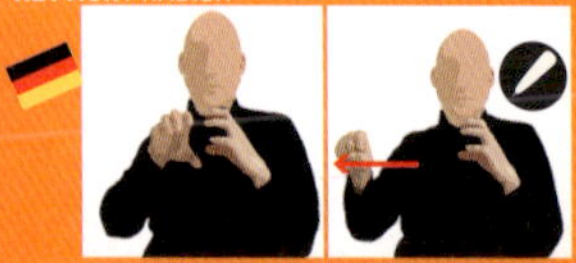

Im Norden wird die Form eines Rettichs gebärdet, in Bayern das Aufschneiden des Radis.
People in the north sign the form of a radish and those in Bavaria sign cutting a radish.

SCHWEINSHAXN / PORK KNUCKLES

BREZE / PRETZEL

MÜNCHEN / MUNICH

Eine Krone für den Ur-Münchner Ludwig I.
A crown, standing for Munich's famous son, Ludwig I

ZUGSPITZE

Der Berg mit dem eigenartigen Gipfel / The mountain with the strangely shaped peak

DIRNDL

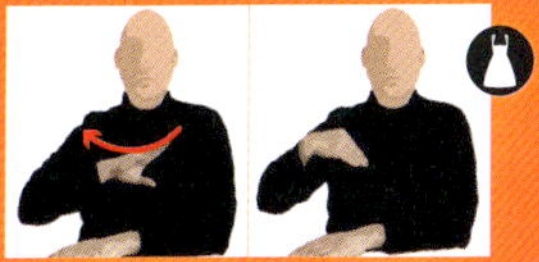

LEDERHOSE

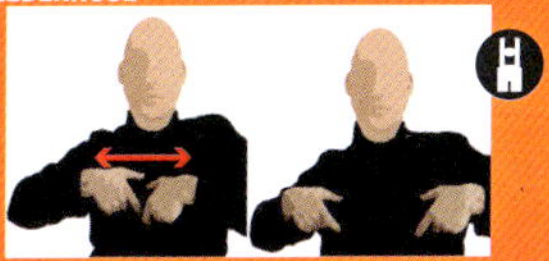

Die Gebärde für den Löwen steht auch für Bayern.
The sign for lion also stands for Bavaria.

BAYERN / BAVARIA

Zum Schluss noch ein dreckiger Witz unter Gehörlosen: die (natürlich falschen) Gebärden für Ober- und Niederbayern.
Finally, a little dirty joke amongst the deaf: the (incorrect, of course) signs for Upper and Lower Bavaria

OBERBAYERN UND NIEDERBAYERN
UPPER BAVARIA AND LOWER BAVARIA

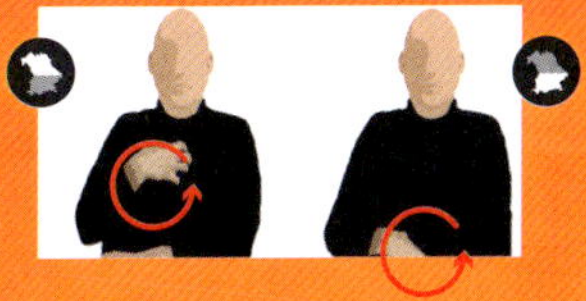

Ja, was glauben sie denn?

You gotta have faith

Die Bayern sind für ihre Frömmigkeit bekannt – sie sind so katholisch, dass sogar die Kurve der Kirchenaustritte aussieht wie ein Gotteshaus. / The Bavarians are renowned for their piousness – they're so Catholic that even the curve mapping those leaving the church looks like a house of God.

Der Papst / The Pope

Benedikt XVI.

*** 1927 in Marktl als** / as
Joseph Aloisius Ratzinger

19.04.2005
Wahl zum ersten deutschen Papst seit 1523
Elected as the first German pope since 1523.

28.02.2013
Amtsverzicht / Resignation

188.936,88 €
erzielte 2005 sein früheres Auto, ein VW Golf, bei einer Versteigerung auf eBa
Price paid in 2005 for his former car, a VW Golf, on eBa

Konfessionen / Confessions

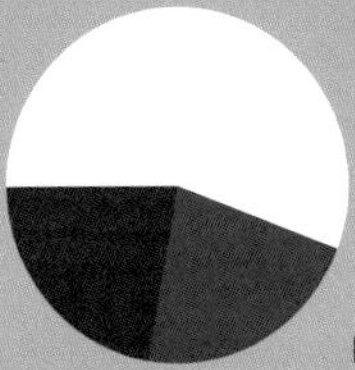

Römisch-katholisch
Roman Catholic
56 %

Evangelisch
Protestant
22 %

Andere
Other
22 %

Altötting

Wallfahrtsort seit mehr als 1250 Jahren
Pilgrimage site for more than 1,250 years

Ziel: „Die schwarze Madonna“
Destination: “The Black Madonna”

> 1 Mio. / mil.
Pilger und Besucher pro Jahr
pilgrims and visitors per year

Austritte aus den bayerischen Bistümern und aus der Evangelisch-Lutherischen Kirche in Bayern

People leaving the Bavarian bisphoprics and the Protestant Church in Bavaria

Missbrauch in katholischen Einrichtungen wird aufgedeckt.
Child abuse in Catholic institutions is exposed.

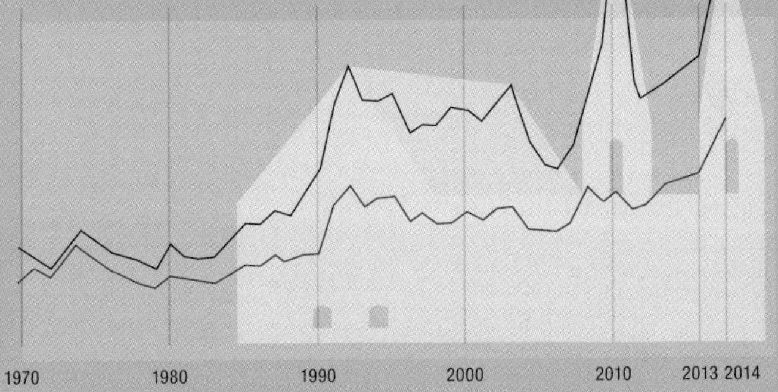

Dom zu Regensburg
Regensburg Cathedral

Katholische Kirche
Catholic Church

Evangelische Kirche
Protestant Church

Wo was los ist
The lay of the land

Wie die Fläche Bayerns genutzt wird – eine flurbereinigte Grafik /
How Bavaria's land is used – a graphic plot

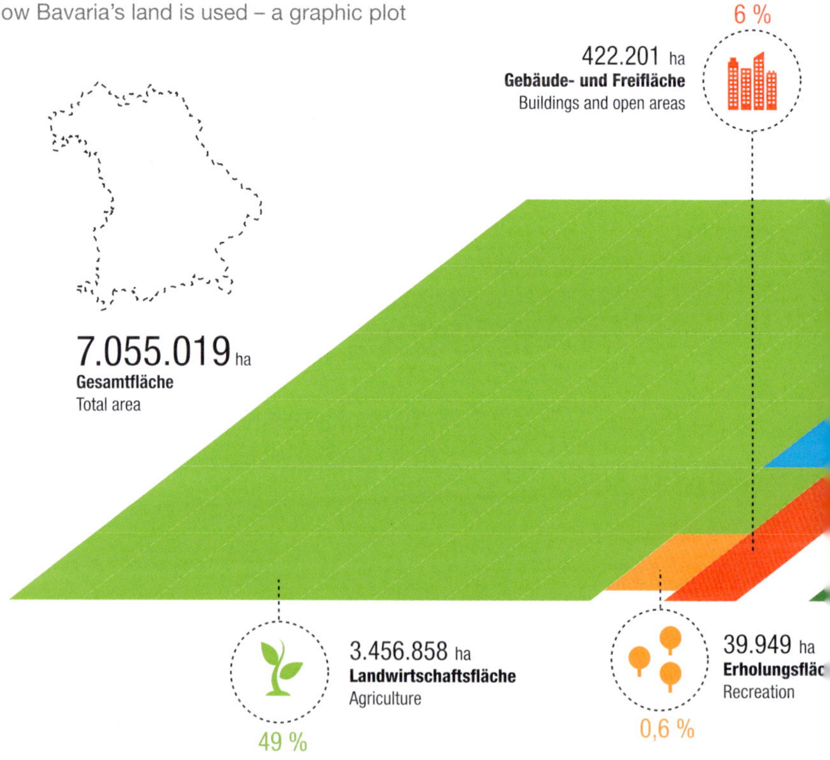

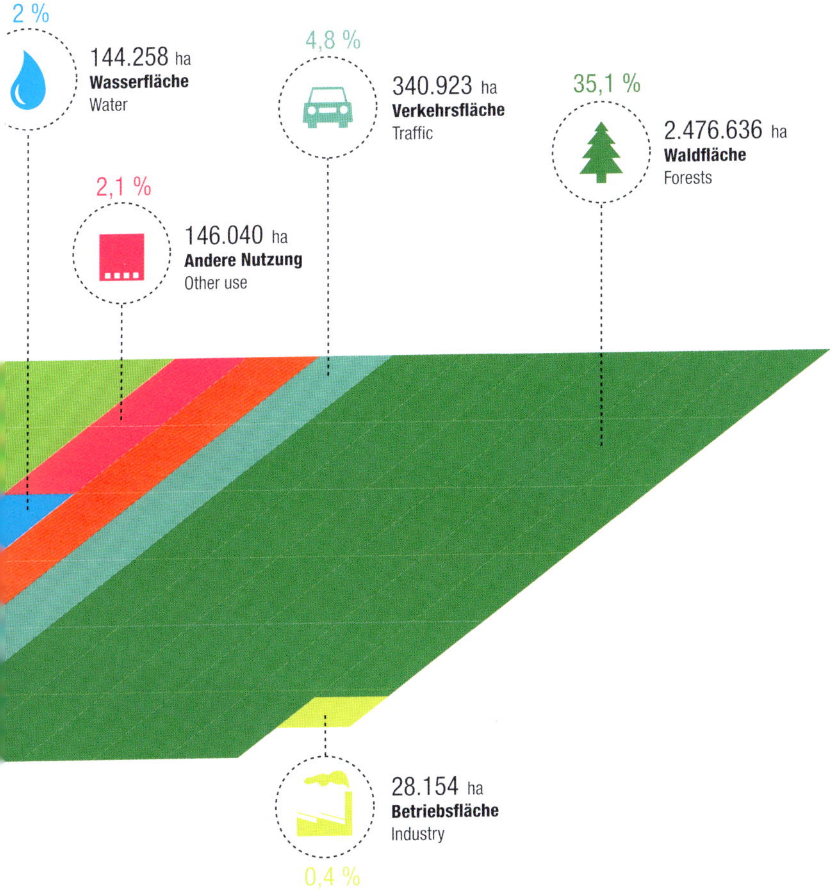
2 %
144.258 ha
Wasserfläche
Water
4,8 %
340.923 ha
Verkehrsfläche
Traffic
35,1 %
2.476.636 ha
Waldfläche
Forests
2,1 %
146.040 ha
Andere Nutzung
Other use
28.154 ha
Betriebsfläche
Industry
0,4 %

Ganz unten, ganz oben
At the bottom, at the top

Der Freistaat hat im föderalistischen Deutschland eine Ausnahmestellung – so oder so.
In federalist Germany, Bavaria is an exception – for better or for worse.

SCHLECHTER ALS DER REST DES LANDES
WORSE THAN IN THE REST OF THE COUNTRY

Stadt mit höchstem Kaufpreis für Eigentumswohnungen: München / City with the highest-pric condominiums: Munich

5.694 € / m²

(2015)

Mieseste Beicht-Quote der Fremdgeher
Poorest confession rate amongst adulterers:
Nur / Only

32 %

berichten dem Partner vom Seitensprung
tell their partner about their affair

Niedrigste Durchschnittstemperat im Frühling (2014)
Lowest average temperature in spring (20

9,5 °C

Bundesdurchschnitt
National average
10,1° C

Meiste Menschen im Gefängnis (relativ zur Bevölkerung)
Most prisoners (relative to the population)

Meiste Pilzvergiftungen
Most mushroom poisonings

26,5 %

aller bundesweit gemeldeten Patienten
of all patients registered nationwide

Beste Förderung des Ökologischen Landbaus
Best promotion of organic farming

Beste Förderung der beruflichen Bildung
Best promotion of vocational education

12

Meiste Feiertage
+ vielerorts Mariä Himmelfahrt
+ Friedensfest in Augsburg
Most holidays
+ in many places the Feast of the Assumption
+ the Augsburg Peace Festival

Höchste Ausgaben für Wurst
Highest expenditure on sausage

372 €

(pro Magen und Jahr / per stomach and year)

Und noch ein Fleißkärtchen für Starnberg: Ort mit höchster Ärzte-Dichte, den meisten nkommensmillionären sowie der längsten Lebenserwartung
nd a special gold star for Starnberg: the town with the highest density of physicians, the most self-made millionaires and the longest life expectancy

Wenigste Straftaten
Fewest crimes

5.164

(je 100.000 Einwohner / per 100,000 inhabitants, **2014**)

Höchste Nachtclub-Dichte
Highest night club density

4,46

(je 100.000 Einwohner / per 100,000 inhabitants**)**

BESSER ALS ALLE ANDEREN BUNDESLÄNDER
BETTER THAN ALL OTHER GERMAN STATES

Die Summe der einzelnen Teile

The sum of the individual parts

Der Freistaat, unendliche Weiten: 2.031 kreisangehörige Gemeinden, 71 Landkreise, 25 kreisfreie Städte – und sieben ziemlich verschiedene Regierungsbezirke / The Free State of Bavaria in all its vastness: 2,031 district towns and municipalities, 71 counties, 25 independent cities – and seven quite diverse administrative districts

- **Fläche** / Area (in km²)
- **Einwohner** / Total population
- **Einwohner** / Population (**je**/per km²)
- **Touristenübernachtungen** Overnight stays by tourists
- **Weinerzeugung** / Wine production (in hl)
- **Schlachtungen** / Livestock slaughtered (in 1.000 / 1,000s)
- **Speisefischerzeugung: Gemeiner Karpfen** Edible fish production: common carp (in t)
- **Einwohner mit Hochschulabschluss** Residents with a university degree
- **Ausländeranteil** / Ratio of foreigners
- **Wohneigentumsquote** Home-ownership rate
- **Katholiken** / Catholics

Regierungssitz / Seat of government

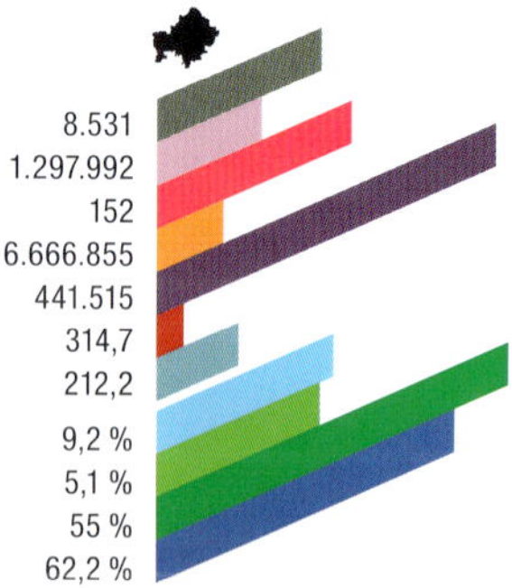

UNTERFRANKEN / LOWER FRANCONIA
Würzburg

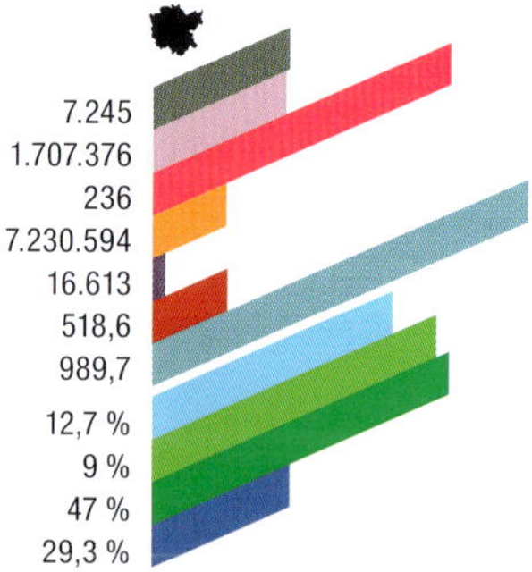

MITTELFRANKEN / MIDDLE FRANCONIA
Ansbach

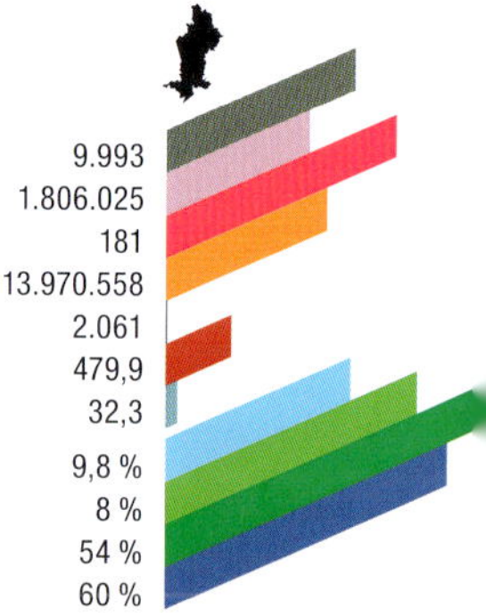

SCHWABEN / SWABIA
Augsburg

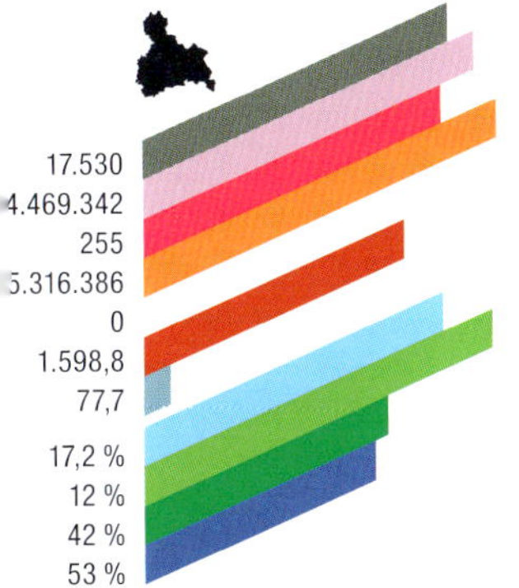

OBERBAYERN / UPPER BAVARIA
München / Munich

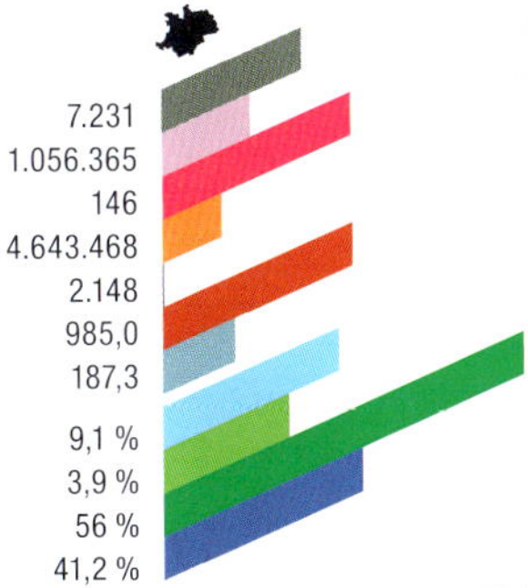

OBERFRANKEN / UPPER FRANCONIA
Bayreuth

BAYERN / BAVARIA
München / Munich

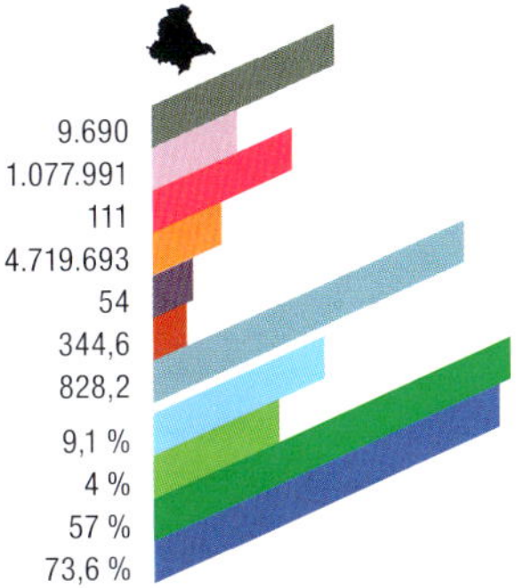

OBERPFALZ / UPPER PALATINATE
Regensburg

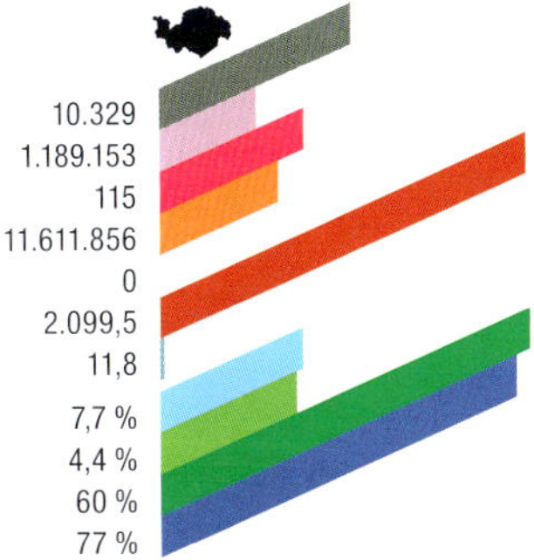

NIEDERBAYERN / LOWER BAVARIA
Landshut

Es war einmal ... der Bajuware
Once upon a time ... the Bajuwars

Die lange Geschichte Bayerns in 18 Sauseschritten /
The long history of Bavaria in 18 quicksteps

1806

Erhebung zum Königreich und Gewinn fränkischer, schwäbischer und österreichischer Gebi
Bavaria is elevated to sta of kingdom and acquir Franconian, Swabian a Austrian territories

1830

Otto I. wird König von Griechenland
Otto I becomes King of Greece

1866

Niederlage gegen die Preußen im Deutschen Krieg
Bavaria is defeated by Prussia in the Prussian-German War

1871

Bayern wird Teil des neu gegründeten Deutschen Reichs
Bavaria becomes part of the newly established German Reich

1918

Ende der Monarchie: Bayern wird „Freistaat", also republikanisch
End of the monarchy: Bavaria becomes a "Free State", i.e. republican

1923

Gescheiterter Hitlerputsch in München, der späteren „Hauptstadt der Bewegung"
Beer Hall Putsch (by Hitler) fails in Munich, later the "Capital of the Movement"

1934

Gleichschaltung Bayer mit dem Reich durch die Nazis
Bavaria is "brought into l with the Reich by the Nazis

555

Erster Beleg eines bairischen Herzogtums nit Sitz in Freising unter den Agilolfingern
First documentation of a Bavarian duchy with seat in Freising under the Agilolfings

1002

Wahl des bayerischen Herzogs Heinrich zum deutschen König
Bavarian Duke Heinrich elected German King

1070–1180

Regentschaft der Welfen (mit Unterbrechungen)
Rule of the Guelfs (with interruptions)

1180–1918

Regentschaft der Wittelsbacher
Rule of the Wittelsbachs

1314

Ludwig der Bayer als erster Wittelsbacher auf dem Kaiserthron
Ludwig the Bavarian is first Wittelsbach on the imperial throne

1506

Wiedervereinigung des Herzogtums nach dem Landshuter Erbfolgekrieg – Primogeniturordnung
Reunification of the duchy after the Landshut War of Succession – primogeniture instituted

1623

Erhebung zum Kurfürstentum
3avaria elevated to
: status of electorate

/erurteilung der Mitglieder der iderstandsgruppe „Weiße Rose“
iction of the members
he resistance group “White Rose”

1946

Volksentscheid über die bayerische Verfassung, Verlust der Rheinpfalz, Wahl von Hans Erhard (CSU) zum Ministerpräsidenten
Referendum on the Bavarian Constitution, loss of the Rhineland-Palatinate, election of Hans Erhard (CSU) as Minister-President

1949

Bayern wird als Bundesland Teil der Bundesrepublik Deutschland.
Bavaria becomes a federal state in the Federal Republic of Germany.

1957

bis in alle Ewigkeit: CSU stellt Ministerpräsidenten.
to eternity: Minister-President comes from the CSU.

Das ist ja die Höhe!
The sky's the limit!

Die höchsten Bauwerke im Freistaat / The tallest buildings in Bavaria

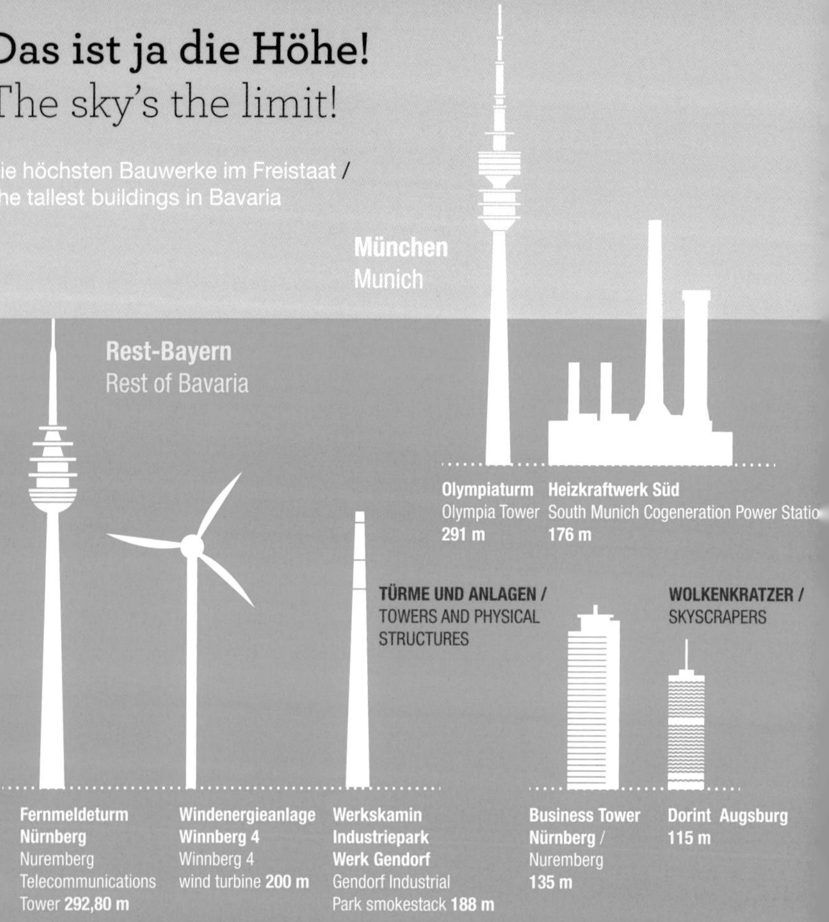

Hier beginnt in München der Himmel:
Seit einem Bürgerentscheid von 2004 dürfen im Stadtgebiet keine Gebäude mehr errichtet werden, die höher sind als die Frauenkirche.
This is where the sky begins in Munich: a public referendum in 2004 put a stop to any new buildings taller than the Church of Our Lady.

Uptown
146 m

Highlight Towers
Highlight Towers
126 m / 113 m

Hypo-Haus
Hypo building
114 m

Frauenkirche
Church of Our Lady
98,57 m

Heilig-Kreuz-Kirche München-Giesing
Holy Cross Church, Munich-Giesing
94,2 m

Höchster Backsteinturm der Welt
World's tallest brick tower

KIRCHEN /
CHURCHES

St. Martin, Landshut
130,6 m

Regensburger Dom
Regensburg Cathedral
104,6 m

Basilika St. Ulrich und Afra Augsburg
Basilica of St. Ulrich and St. Afra, Augsburg
93 m

Dem Himmel so nah

So close to heaven

Böse Zungen behaupten ja, die schönsten Berge der deutschen Alpen lägen in Österreich – der Gipfel der Frechheit. Hier sind 10 + 1 Gegenbeweise aus Oberbayern und Schwaben. / Malicious rumours have it that the most beautiful mountains in the German Alps are in Austria – the height of impertinence. Here are 10 + 1 proofs to the contrary from Upper Bavaria and Swabia.

Kraxelnde Sehenswürdigkeiten: d Huberbuam. Tipp: Immer nach ob schauen! / Clambering attractions: the extreme-climbing Huber brother Tip: Always look up!

Zugspitze 2.962 m

Deutschlands höchste und bebauteste Spitze
Germany's highest and most developed peak

Watzmann 2.713 m

2014 zum „Schönsten Berg der Welt“ gewählt
Elected “Most Beautiful Mountain in the World” in 2014

Hochkalter 2.607 m

Leckerster Kuchen der Alpen auf der Blaueishütte
Most delicious cake in the Alps at the Blaueishütte cabin

Trettachspitze 2.595 m

Das Allgäuer Matterhorn
The Matterhorn of the Allgäu region

Höfats 2.259 m

Ein Edelweiß-Paradies
An Edelweiss paradise

Die höchsten Berge der anderen Regierungsbezirke
The highest mountains in the other administrative districts

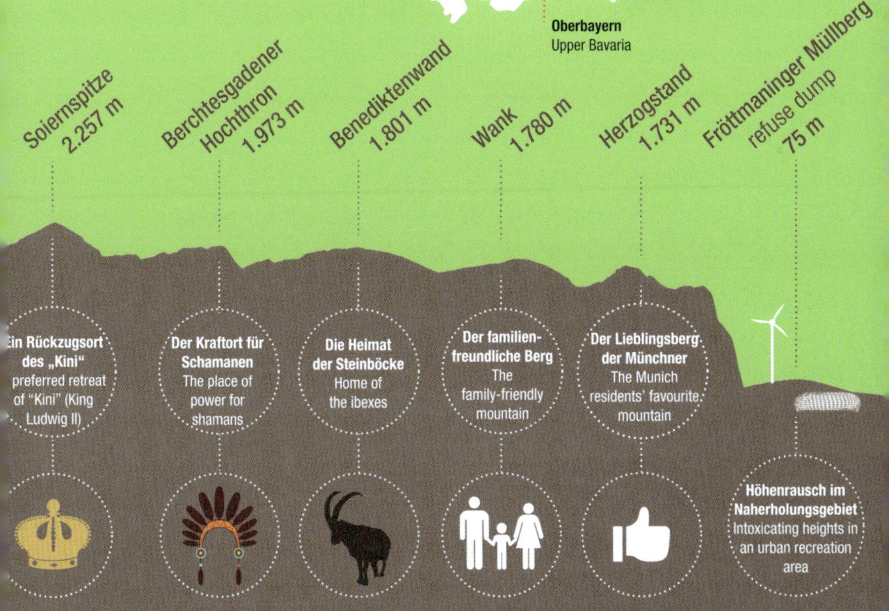

Was braucht man Meer?
All there is to sea

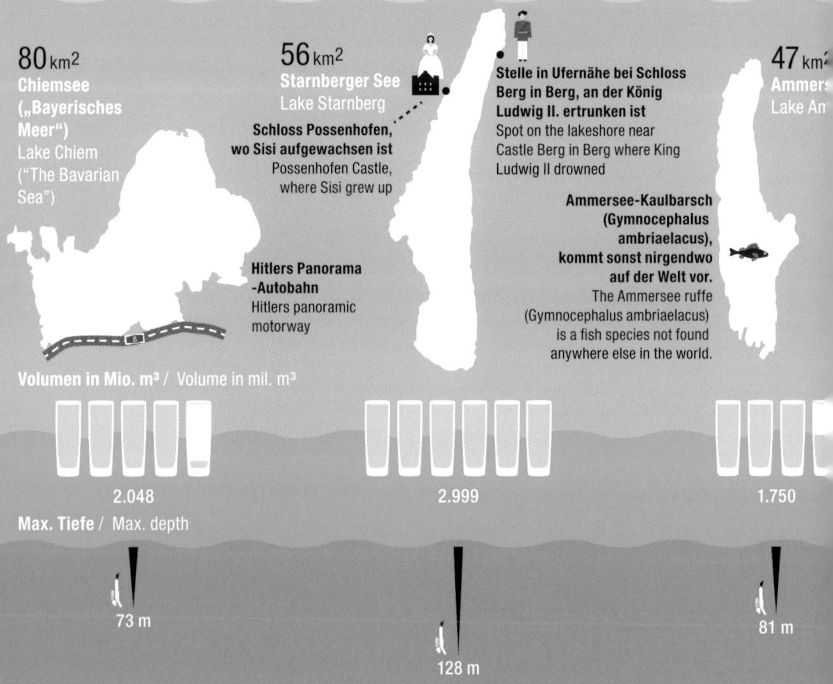

Stille Wasser sind tief: die zehn größten Seen in Bayern / Still waters run deep: the ten largest lakes in Bavaria

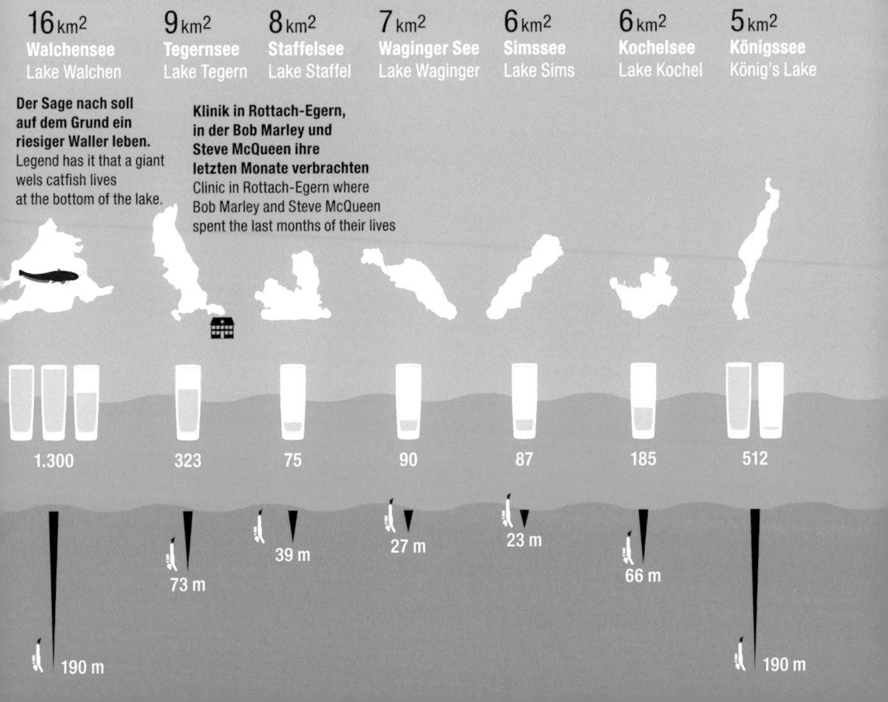

Waldmeisterschaft
Sylvan supremacy

Das ist ja wohl der Wipfel: Bayerns Bäume /
Hard to top: Bavaria's trees

Die Eigentümer der Wälder /
Owners of the forests

Staatswald (Wald des Freistaats Bayern)
Bavarian State Forest
(Forest of the Free State of Bavaria)

Körperschaftswald
Publicly owned forest

Bundeswald
National Forest

Privatwald
Private forest

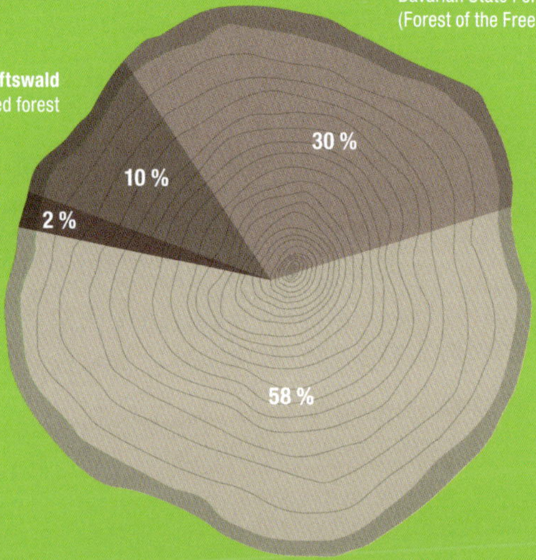

1 m³
Zuwachs pro Sekunde
Growth per second

700.000
Waldbesitzer/-innen
forest owners

44 %
Fichte
spruce
5.000.000.000 Bäume / trees
19 %
Kiefer
pine
12 %
Buche
beech
6 %
Eiche
oak
2 %
Tanne
fir
2 %
Lärche
larch
1 %
Douglasie
Douglas fir
14 %
Sonstige
others

Aufs Korn genommen

In their sights

Mit Gewehr: Jagdszenen aus Niederbayern (und dem Rest des Freistaats) /
On their game: Hunting scenes from Lower Bavaria (and the rest of the state)

DER WILDSCHÜTZ / THE POACHER
GEORG „GIRGL“ JENNERWEIN

42.600
Jäger
hunters

3.40
Jägerinn
huntress

Abschüsse pro Jahr / Kills per year

307.411	112.996	98.163	80.080	65.718	22.162	16.135
Rehwild Roe deer	**Fuchs** Fox	**Stockente** Mallard duck	**Feldhase** Hare	**Schwarzwild** Wild boar	**Fasan** Pheasant	**Dachs** Badger

Geschützte Wildtiere
Protected wild animals

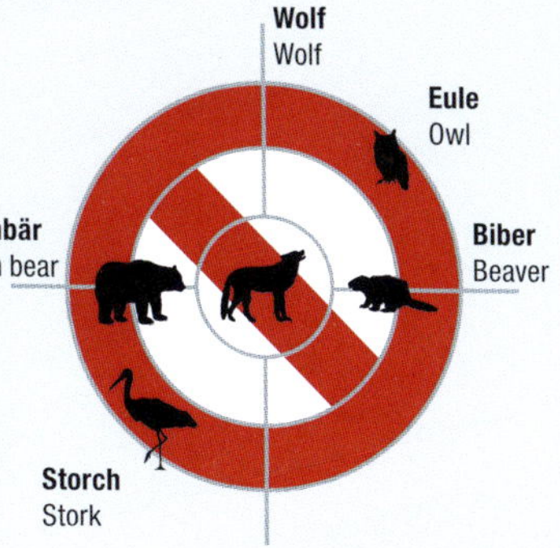

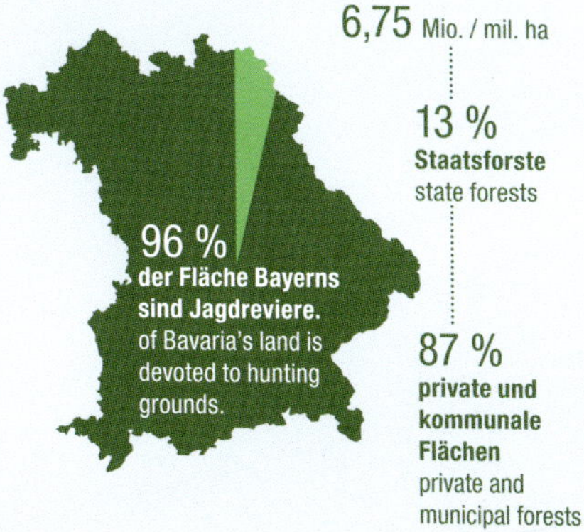

2.532 + 1.500	12.526	7.533	6.059	4.447	3.914
ein- und Baummarder	**Rotwild**	**Wildkaninchen**	**Grau- und Kanadagans**	**Gamswild**	**Iltis, Hermelin, Mauswiesel**
one and pine martens	Red deer	Wild rabbits	Grey and Canada goose	Chamois	Polecat, stoat, weasel

Einer für alle, alle in einem
One for all, all for one

Hätten Sie gerne ein Fabelwesen als Haustier? Einen *Wolpertinger* vielleicht? Dann stellen Sie sich doch einen zusammen! Hier finden Sie animalisches Material zum Ausschneiden, frei nach Albrecht Dürer. / How would you like to have your very own mythical creature as a pet? A *Wolpertinger* perhaps? Then just put one together to suit your taste! Here is plenty of animal material for you to work with, following in the footsteps of Albrecht Dürer.

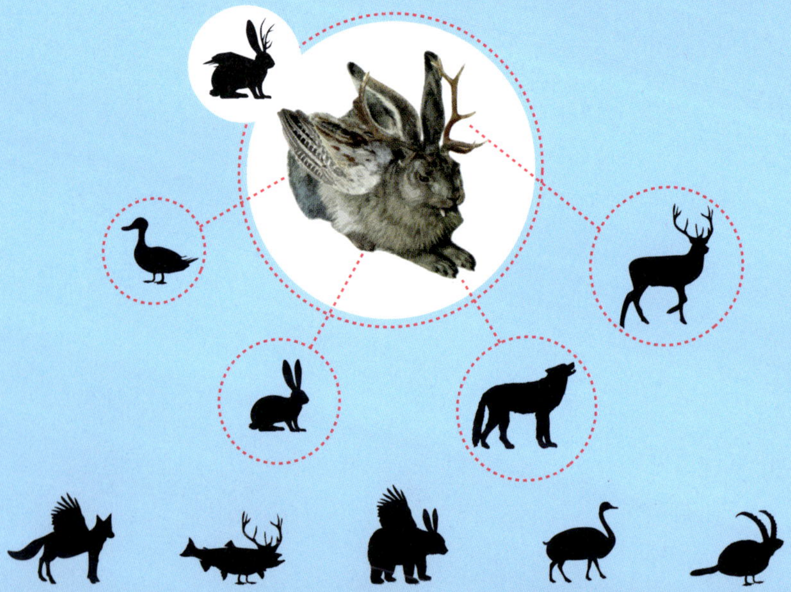

... die größten Kartoffeln

... the biggest potatoes

Die Landwirtschaft in Bayern – ein Bauerzustand /
Farming in Bavaria – the order of the day

HOFBERICHTERSTATTUNG
THE FARM REPORT

Zahl der Höfe
Number of farms

1979	274.273
1999	154.189
2010	97.735

SUBVENTIONEN
SUBSIDIES

1,04 **Milliarden** / billion €

erhielten die Agrarbetriebe in Bayern 2013 insgesamt an EU-Subventionen.
in EU subsidies were received by agricultural operations in Bavaria in 2013.

ÖKOLOGISCHER LANDBAU
ORGANIC FARMING

7.300
Betriebe / operations
230.000 ha

Anteil der Biomilch in Molkereien
Ratio of organic milk produced by dairies

4,8 %

Anteil der Bio-Tiere an Bayerns Gesamtbestand
Ratio of organically raised livestock in Bavaria's agricultural operations

5,6 %
Rinder / cattle

0,8 %
Schweine / pigs

5,8 %
Geflügel / poultry

9,5 %
Schafe / sheep

40,7 %
Ziegen / goats

DAS LIEBE VIEH
LIVESTOCK

3.230.500
Rinder, Kühe und Kälber
steers, cows and calves

Eine Milchkuh gibt 7.697 kg Milch pro Jah
A milk cow produces 7.697 kg milk per year.

3.356.600
Schweine und Zuchtsauen
pigs and breeding sows

4.160.000
Legehennen
laying hens

1.220.000.000
Eier pro Jahr
eggs per year

NUTZUNG DER LANDWIRTSCHAFTSFLÄCHE / USE OF AGRICULTURAL LAND

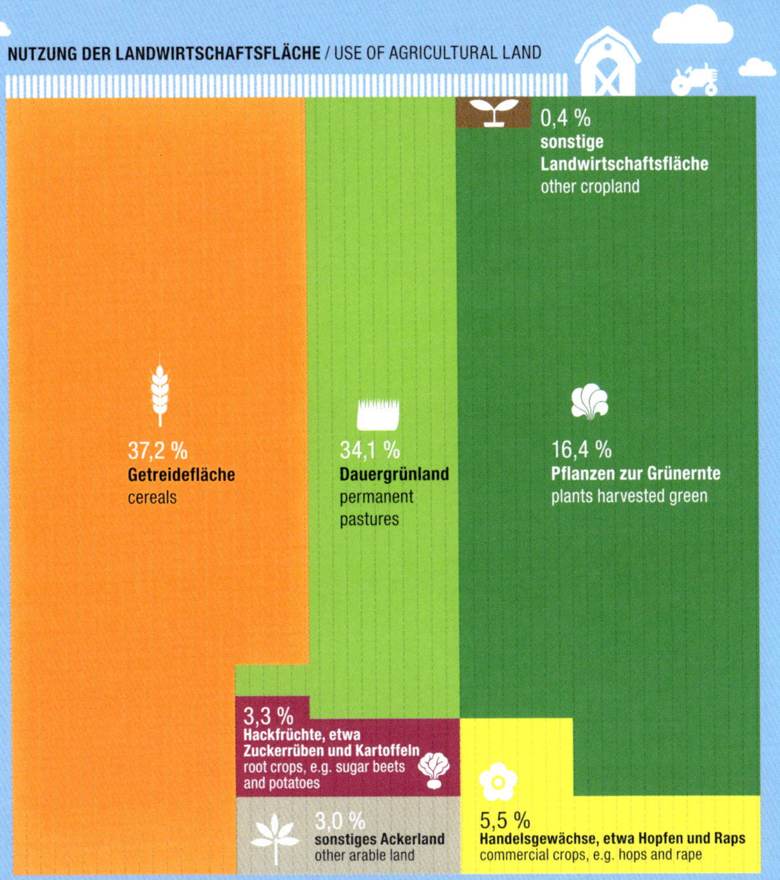

An guadn!
Enjoy!

Aufgebrezelt: Bayerische Erzeugnisse unter EU-Schutz / Pepped up: Bavarian products under EU protection

HEIMATLICHES SPEISEWISSEN / REGIONAL FOOD LORE

Erfinder / Inventor
Anton Nepomuk Pfannenbrenner
11.02.1839
Erstverkaufstag / First day of sale

1516
Erlass des Bayerischen Reinheitsgebots durch Herzog Wilhelm IV. von Bayern: Ins Bier gehören nur Gerste, Hopfen und Wasser. / Wiliam IV, Duke of Bavaria, issues the well-known Bavarian Purity Law: beer should be made only of barley, hops and water.

24.6.
Ende der Spargelsaison („Kirschen rot, Spargel tot.")
End of the asparagus season ("The cherry is red, and the asparagus is dead.")

September–April
Karpfen werden nur in den Monaten mit „r" angeboten – in Franken zumeist gebacken.
Carps are offered only in the months with "r" – in Franconia mostly baked

---

geschützte geographische Angabe (g.g.A.)
protected geographical indication (PGI)

geschützte Ursprungsbezeichnung (g.U.)
protected designation of origin (PDO)

2014

Bayerische Brezn
Bavarian pretzel

1998

Schwäbisch-Hällisches Qualitätsschweinefleisch
Swabian-Hall quality pork

2010
Hopfen aus der Hallertau
Hops from the Hallertau

2012
Spalter Hopfen
Spalt hops

2013
Bamberger Hörnla
Bamberg potato

2007
Bayerischer Meerrettich
Bavarian horseradish

2009
Schwäbische Maultaschen
Swabian Maultaschen

2012
Schwäbische Spätzle
Swabian spaetzle

2001
Bayerisches Bier
Bavarian beer

1998
Kulmbacher Bier
Kulmbach beer

1998
Mainfranken Bier
Mainfranken beer

2010
Münchener Bier
Munich beer

1998
Reuther Bier
Reuth beer

1998
Hofer Bier
Hof beer

2011
ofer Rindfleischwurst
Hof beef sausage

2003
Nürnberger Rostbratwürste
Nuremberg bratwursts

2011
Bayerisches Rindfleisch
Bavarian beef

1997
Allgäuer Bergkäse
Allgäu mountain cheese

1997
Allgäuer Emmentaler
Allgäu Emmental cheese

1996
Nürnberger Lebkuchen
Nuremberg gingerbread

2012
Abensberger Spargel
Abensberg asparagus

2013
Fränkischer Spargel
Franconian asparagus

2010
Schrobenhausener Spargel
Schrobenhausen asparagus

2012
Aischgründer Karpfen
Aischgrund carp

2012
Franken-Karpfen
Franconian carp

2002
Oberpfälzer Karpfen
Upper Palatinate carp

Schwarzbuch Weißwurst
The black book on the white sausage

Weil es eben nicht wurst ist, was in der Wurst ist: Wie die Leibspeise der Bayern gemacht und gegessen wird (nach Münchens bestem Metzger, Magnus Bauch) / Because only the best is good enough for the wurst, here's how Bavaria's favourite food is made and eaten (according to Munich's top butcher, Magnus Bauch)

Wie man die Weißwurst isst / How to eat white sausage

1 **Mit der Gabel anstechen,**
Pierce with fork,

2 **einmal quer in der Mitte durchschneiden,**
cut in half crosswise,

3 **Wursthälften der Länge nac aufschneiden,**
cut each half dc the middle lengthwise,

4 **mit der Gabel aus der Pelle z und essen.**
pull out of casin with fork and ea

5 **Dazu Weißbier, Brezen und süßer Senf.**
Ideal with wheat beer, pretzels and sweet mustard.

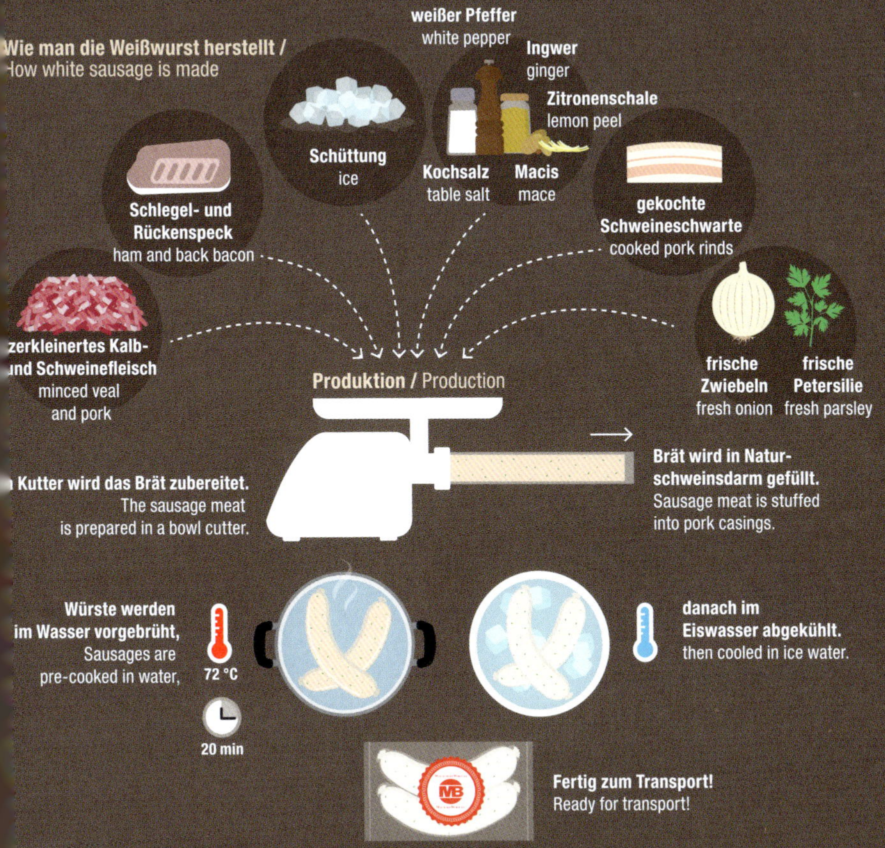
Wie man die Weißwurst herstellt /
How white sausage is made
Schlegel- und Rückenspeck
ham and back bacon
Schüttung
ice
weißer Pfeffer
white pepper
Ingwer
ginger
Zitronenschale
lemon peel
Kochsalz
table salt
Macis
mace
gekochte Schweineschwarte
cooked pork rinds
zerkleinertes Kalb- und Schweinefleisch
minced veal and pork
frische Zwiebeln
fresh onion
frische Petersilie
fresh parsley
Produktion / Production
Kutter wird das Brät zubereitet.
The sausage meat is prepared in a bowl cutter.
Brät wird in Naturschweinsdarm gefüllt.
Sausage meat is stuffed into pork casings.
Würste werden im Wasser vorgebrüht,
Sausages are pre-cooked in water,
72 °C
20 min
danach im Eiswasser abgekühlt.
then cooled in ice water.
Fertig zum Transport!
Ready for transport!

Bier gewinnt
There's nothing like beer!

Kein Volk dieser Erde ist so stolz auf seine Lieblingsdroge wie die Bayern auf ihren Gerstensaft. Und das auch noch mit Recht. Prost! / No people on earth is as proud of its favourite drug as the Bavarians are of their beer. And you can't blame them. Cheers!

BAYERISCHER GESAMTBIERAUSSTOSS 2014
TOTAL BAVARIAN BEER PRODUCTION IN 2014

24,9 **Mio.** / mil. **hl**

1,8 **Mio.** / mil. **hl**
alkoholfreies Bier
non-alcoholic beer

23,1 **Mio.** / mil. **hl**
Vollbier
Vollbier (11 to 14% extra

18,5 Mio. / mil. **hl**
Bayerischer Gesamtbierabsatz im Inland 2014
Total domestic sales of Bavarian beer in 2014

4,6 Mio. / mil. **hl**
im Ausland
sold abroad

Damit könnte man die Allianz-Arena zu 82 % füllen.
This quantity would fill 82% of the Allianz Arena.

ERTEILUNG DER DREI BELIEBTESTEN SORTEN
STRIBUTION OF THE THREE MOST POPULAR
ER TYPES

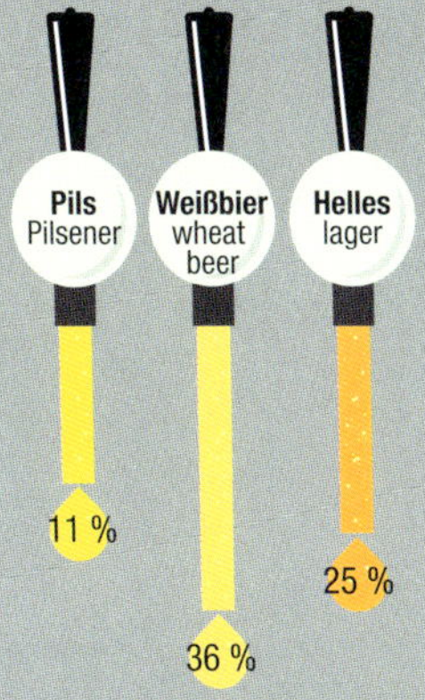

ENERGIE
ENERGY

43 kcal **100 ml**
Bier / beer

31 kcal **100 ml**
alkoholfreies Bier
non-alcoholic beer

Der Gesamtbierabsatz Bayerns 2014 könnte vom Nährwert her theoretisch mehr als 1,14 Millionen Menschen ein Jahr lang ernähren – mehr als alle erwachsenen Münchner.
The total Bavarian beer sales in 2014 could theoretically feed 1.14 million people for one year – more than the entire adult population of Munich.

23.4. **Tag des deutschen Bieres**
German Beer Day

135–215 l
chätzter durchschnittlicher rkonsum pro Kopf pro Jahr ei über 16-jährigen Bayern)
ated average per capita beer nsumption per year (amongst varians over 16 years of age)

BRAUEREIEN NACH BUNDESLÄNDERN
BREWERIES BY FEDERAL STATE

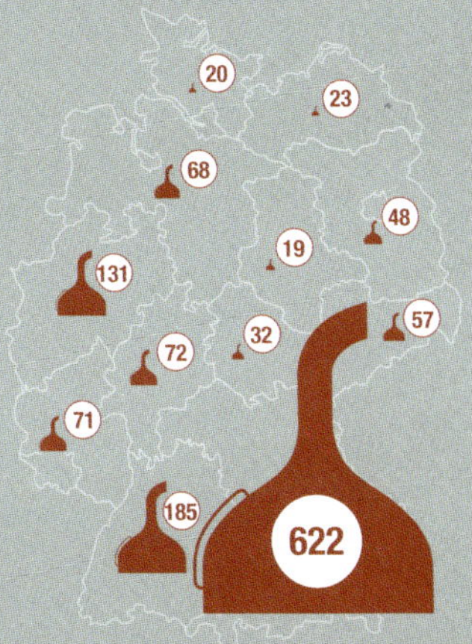

Im Land der Schenkelklopfer

In the land of the knee slappers

Mit dem Schuhplattler, traditionell in Tracht aufgeführt, buhlten die Tänzer einst um die Herzen ihrer Angebeteten – heute erobern sie damit vor allem die der Touristen. / With the Schuhplattler dance, traditionally performed in folk costume, men once courted their sweethearts – and today conquer the hearts of tourists.

Im Paradiesgarten
In the Garden of Eden

Alles außer Äpfel und Schlangen: Was einen Biergarten zu einem Biergarten macht. / Everything but apples and snakes: What makes a beer garden a beer garden?

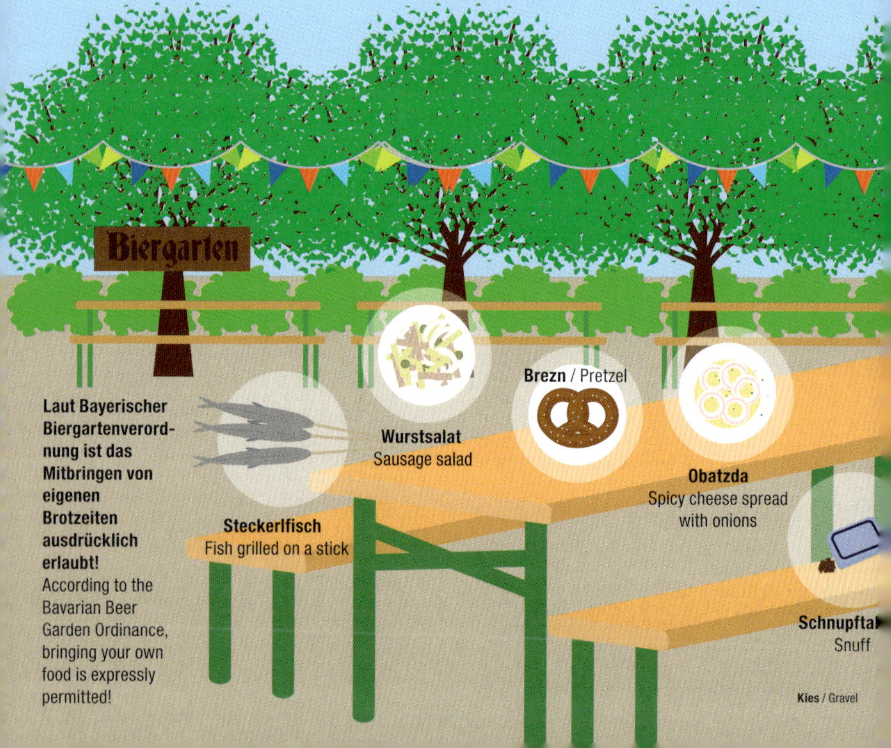

Laut Bayerischer Biergartenverordnung ist das Mitbringen von eigenen Brotzeiten ausdrücklich erlaubt!
According to the Bavarian Beer Garden Ordinance, bringing your own food is expressly permitted!

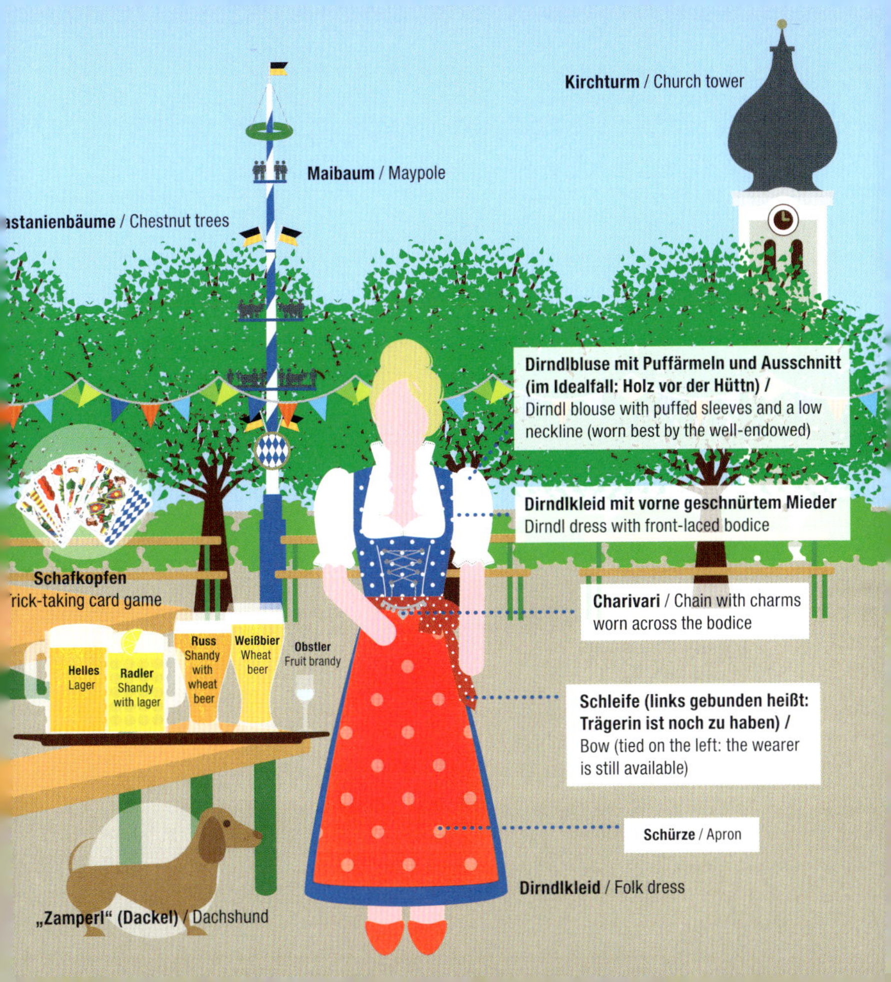

Kirchturm / Church tower
Maibaum / Maypole
astanienbäume / Chestnut trees
Dirndlbluse mit Puffärmeln und Ausschnitt (im Idealfall: Holz vor der Hüttn) / Dirndl blouse with puffed sleeves and a low neckline (worn best by the well-endowed)
Dirndlkleid mit vorne geschnürtem Mieder
Dirndl dress with front-laced bodice
Schafkopfen
rick-taking card game
Charivari / Chain with charms worn across the bodice
Helles
Lager
Radler
Shandy with lager
Russ
Shandy with wheat beer
Weißbier
Wheat beer
Obstler
Fruit brandy
Schleife (links gebunden heißt: Trägerin ist noch zu haben) / Bow (tied on the left: the wearer is still available)
Schürze / Apron
Dirndlkleid / Folk dress
„Zamperl" (Dackel) / Dachshund

O'zapft is!

Bottoms up!

Maßlos maßvoll: zwei Wochen lang die größte Party der Welt, das Oktoberfest / Barrels of fun: for two weeks the biggest party in the world, the Oktoberfest

BIERAUSSCHANK IN DEN GROSSEN BIERZELTEN
BEER SERVED IN THE BIG BEER TENTS:

Wochentags
Weekdays
10–22:30 **Uhr** / h

Samstags und an Sonn- und Feiertagen
Saturday, Sunday and holidays
9–22:30 **Uhr** / h

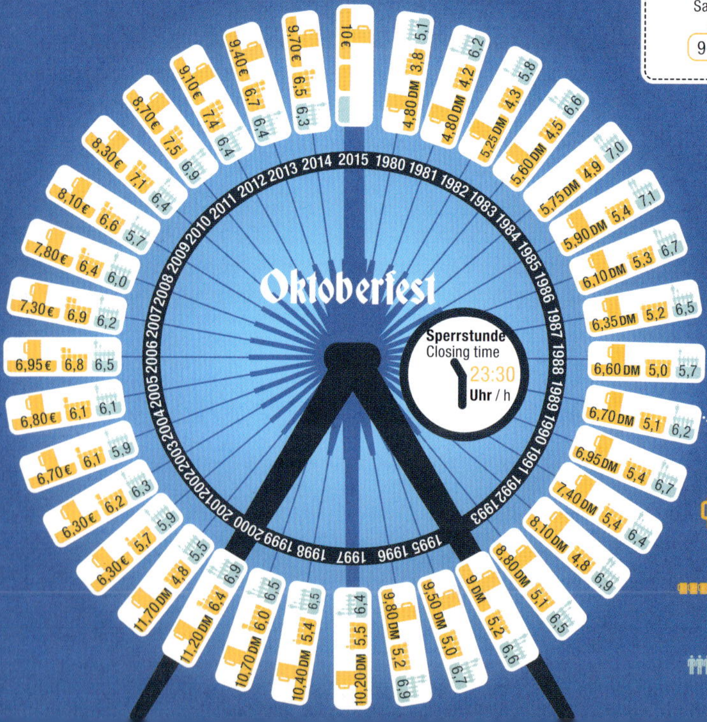

Preis der billigste
Maß (1 l) in DM bz
(ab 2002) in €
Price of the cheape
beer (1 l) in DM or
(from 2002) in €

Bierkonsum (in Mio. l)
Beer consumption (in mil. l)

Besucher (in Mio.
Visitors (in mil.)

Oktober / October 1810

1. Oktoberfest anlässlich der Hochzeit von Kronprinz Ludwig und Prinzessin Therese
1st Oktoberfest celebrating the wedding of Crown Prince Ludwig and Princess Therese

Infrastruktur / Infrastructure

31 ha
Fläche
floor area

14
große Zelte
big tents

8.000
Festangestellte
permanent staff members

21
kleine Zelte
small tents

4.000
wechselnde Arbeitskräfte
temporary workers

107.000
Sitzplätze
seats

95
Gastronomiebetriebe
food establishments

60
Flöhe im Flohzirkus
fleas in the flea circus

80
Fahrgeschäfte
amusement park rides

878 m
Toiletten-Stehplätze
of pissoirs

26
behindertengerechte Toiletten
disabled toilets

964
Toiletten-Sitzplätze
toilet seats

15 %
der Maßkrüge sind nicht voll eingeschenkt (Unterschank).
of the beer mugs are not completely filled.

15 mm
Unterschank sind erlaubt.
empty space from the top of the beer mug is allowed.

1,5 s
durchschnittliche Einschankzeit für eine Maß
average filling time for a one-litre mug

112.000
Bierkrüge wurden 2014 den Andenkenjägern abgenommen.
beer mugs were reclaimed from souvenir hunters in 2014.

Kuriosa / Curiosities

Berühmtester Hilfsarbeiter auf der Wiesn
Most famous worker at the Wiesn
Albert Einstein

Der Münchner Oberbürgermeister zapft traditionell das erste Bierfass an und läutet damit den Beginn der Wiesn ein.
Munich's Lord Mayor traditionally taps the first barrel, kicking off the beginning of the Oktoberfest.

Größter Fauxpas („Izapft os" statt „Ozapft is")
Biggest faux pas (He said "Izapft os" instead of "Ozapft is"): **Erich Kiesl** (1978)

Schnellster Anzapfer / Fastest barrel tapper
Christian Ude (2 Schläge / strikes**, 2009)**

„2 Maß sind nicht zu viel für Autofahrer."
"2 litres of beer is not too much for a driver."
(Günther Beckstein, ehemaliger Ministerpräsident former Prime Minister of Bavaria, **2008)**

Einmal Wagner, immer Wagner
Once Wagner, always Wagner

Richard Wagner
BAYREUTHER FESTSPIELE

29.04.1872
1. Spatenstich Festspielgebäude
Ground-breaking for festival building

13.08.1876
Beginn der ersten Festspiele
First festival commences

1.937
Sitzplätze
seats

730 m²
Hauptbühne
main stage

10–320 €
Eintrittskarte
Ticket price

30
Vorstellungen pro Jahr
performances per year

Richard Wagner
*** 22.05.1813 in Leipzig**
† 13.02.1883
in Venedig / Venice

140 m²
Orchestergraben
orchestra pit

110
Musiker
musicians

DER KANZLERIN NEUE KLEIDER / THE CHANCELLOR'S NEW CLOTHES

1999 2000 2001 2002 2003 2004 2005 2007

Die Festspiele in Bayreuth sind jedes Jahr ein großes Schaulaufen der Prominenz. Nebenbei läuft noch Musik: die zehn letzten Opern Richard Wagners / The festival in Bayreuth is THE place for celebrities to see and be seen each year. And then there's the music of course: Richard Wagner's last ten completed operas.

EITUNG DER FESTSPIELE / FESTIVAL DIRECTORS

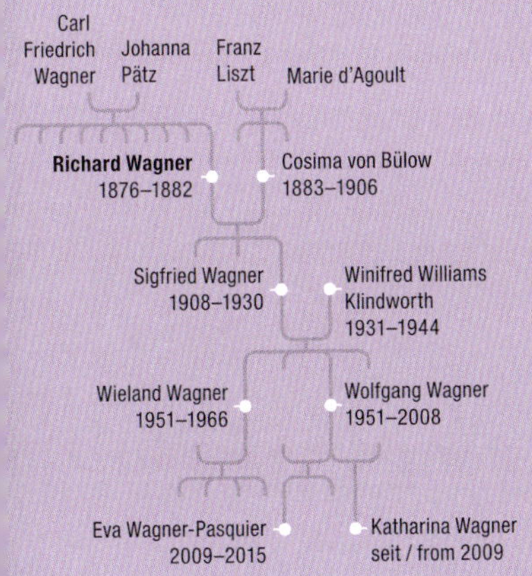

Spielplan / Programme

Der fliegende Holländer
The Flying Dutchman

...

Tannhäuser

...

Lohengrin

...

Der Ring des Nibelungen (Das Rheingold, Die Walküre, Siegfried, Götterdämmerung)
The Ring of the Nibelung (The Rhine Gold, The Valkyrie, Siegfried, Twilight of the Gods)

...

Tristan und Isolde

...

Die Meistersinger von Nürnberg
The Master-Singers of Nuremberg

...

Parsifal

---

9. Sinfonie (Beethoven)
Symphony No. 9 (Beethoven)

Stammgast Angela Merkel kommt jedesmal in einer anderen Robe. Fast jedesmal.
Regular festival guest Angela Merkel dons a new gown every time. Or almost every time.

Gehst du her do!
You – get over here!

Kein schöner Land: Bayern als Urlaubsziel /
No land more lovely: Bavaria as holiday destination

Wo die ausländischen Besucher herkommen:
Where foreign visitors come from:

(Millionen Übernachtungen / in millions of overnight stays)

1,5	**USA**
1,4	**Niederlande** Netherlands
1,4	**Österreich** Austria
1,3	**Schweiz** Switzerland
1,2	**Italien** Italy
1,0	**Vereinigtes Königreich** United Kingdom
0,8	**Russland** Russia
0,8	**Arabische Golfstaaten** Arab Gulf States
0,6	**Frankreich** France

32,5 Mio. / mil.
Ankünfte pro Jahr / arrivals per year

76 %
Inländer
Germans

24 %
Ausländer
foreigners

85,2 Mio. / mil.
Nächtigungen pro Jahr
overnight stays per year

2,6
Tage / days
bleibt ein Tourist durchschnittlich im Land.
Length of the average tourist stay

nzahl Touristen nach egierungsbezirk pro Jahr

umber of tourists per administrative strict per year

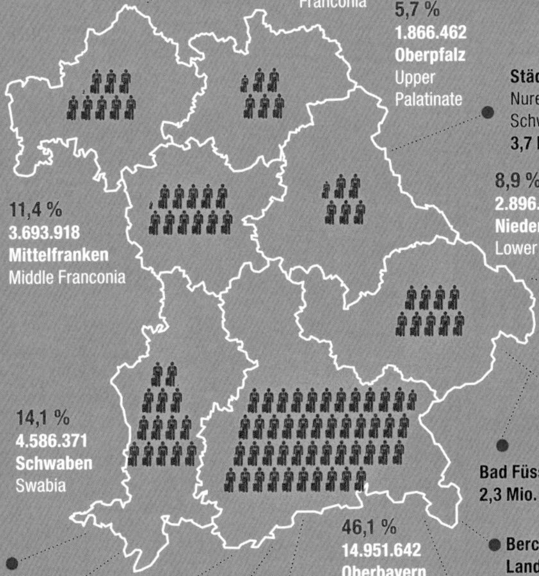

Im Auftrag Ihrer Majestät
By order of Your Majesty

König Ludwig II. hat nicht nur luxuriös gewohnt, sondern auch herrschaftlich bauen lassen. Nicht umsonst heißt der Kerl „Märchenkönig". / King Ludwig II not only lived in the lap of luxury — he also commissioned a series of opulent residences, earning him the nickname "The Fairytale King".

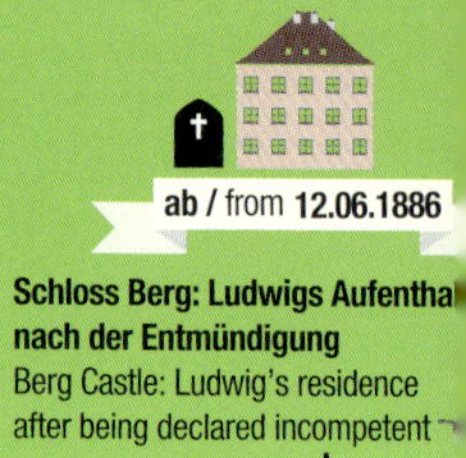

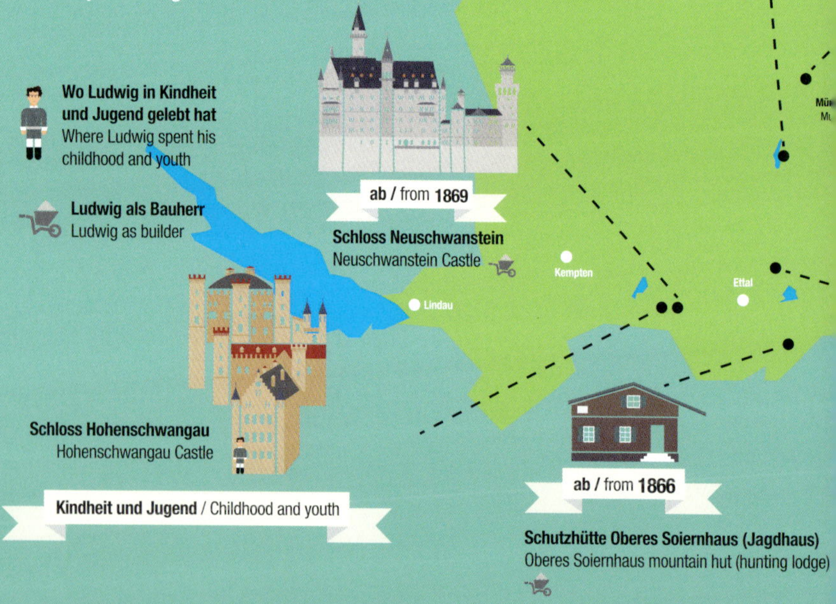

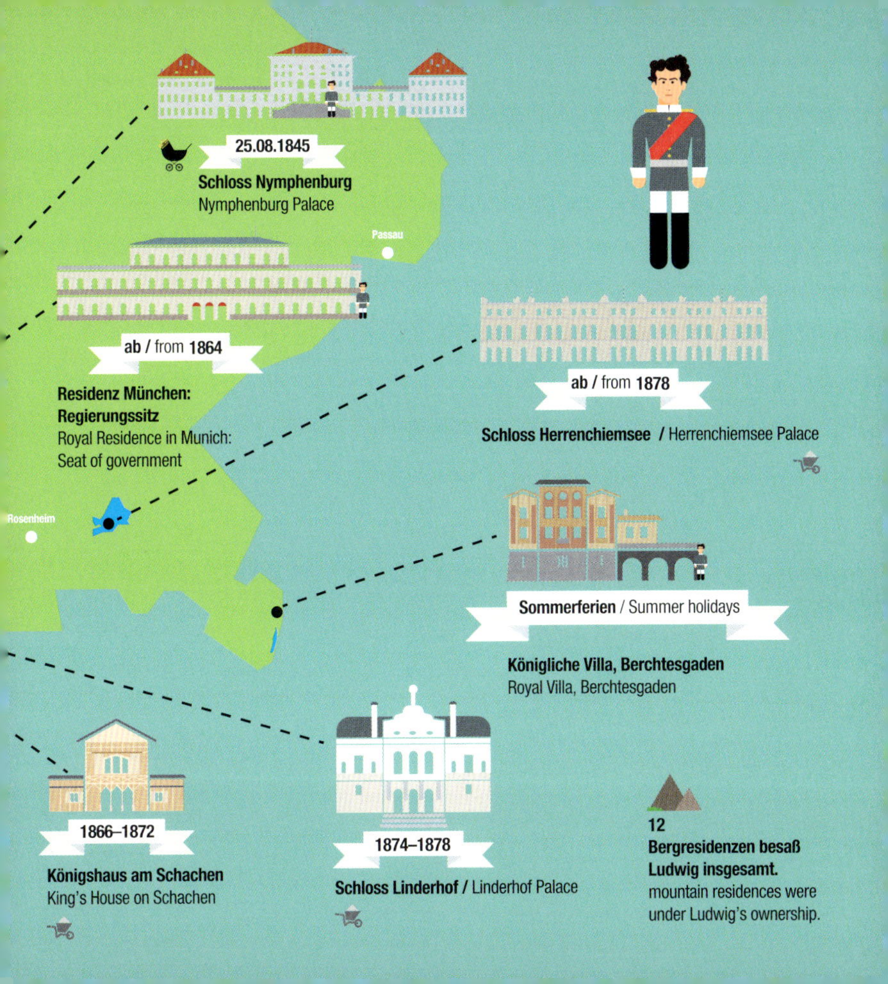

25.08.1845
Schloss Nymphenburg
Nymphenburg Palace
Passau
ab / from 1864
Residenz München:
Regierungssitz
Royal Residence in Munich:
Seat of government
Rosenheim
ab / from 1878
Schloss Herrenchiemsee / Herrenchiemsee Palace
Sommerferien / Summer holidays
Königliche Villa, Berchtesgaden
Royal Villa, Berchtesgaden
1866–1872
Königshaus am Schachen
King's House on Schachen
1874–1878
Schloss Linderhof / Linderhof Palace
12
Bergresidenzen besaß
Ludwig insgesamt.
mountain residences were
under Ludwig's ownership.

Königlich-kaiserlich
Royal-Imperial

Kaiser im 20. Jahrhundert
Emperor in the 20th century

FRANZ ANTON BECKENBAUER

1945
München Giesing

Eltern / Parents:
Postobersekretär Franz sen. & Antonie (geb. Hupfauf)
Postal worker Franz sen. & Antonie (née Hupfauf)

Jugend / Youth:
SC 1906 München

Thomas

1. Spiel für den FC Bayern
1st match played for FC Bayern

1. Werbevertrag (Knorr Fertigsuppen)
1st advertising contract (Knorr instant soups)

1. von 4 DFB-Pokalen
1st of 4 DFB (German Football Association) Cups

Brig.
Witt.

Mi

'45 — '61 — '62 — '63 — '64 — '66

LUDWIG II

König im 19. Jahrhundert
King in the 19th century

1845
Schloss Nymphenburg
Nymphenburg Palace

Eltern / Parents:
Kronprinz Maximilian & Kronprinzessin Marie
Crown Prince Maximilian & Crown Princess Marie

Jugend / Youth:
Schloss Hohenschwangau
Hohenschwangau Palace

Sieht Richard Wagners Opern
Sees Richard Wagner's operas

Beginnt Studium an der Münchner Universität: Physik, Chemie, Logik und Geschichte der Philosophie
Begins studies at Munich University: physics, chemistry, logic and history of philosophy

† König Maximilian: Ludwig wird König von Bayern
† King Maximilian: Ludwig becomes King of Bavaria

Trifft / Meets
Richard Wagner.

Schickt B
an der Se
Österreic
den Deuts
Krieg – u
verliert.
Sends Bav
war on Au
side – and
defeated.

'67

Spitzname „Der Kaiser"
Nickname "The Emperor"

Verlobung mit Sophie, der Schwester von Kaiserin Sisi. Später Entlobung.
Engaged to Sophie, sister of Empress Sisi. Later broken off.

'68

Stefan

Gründet heutige *Technische Universität München.*
Founds today's *Technische Universität München.*

'69

1. von 5 Deutschen Meisterschaften
1st of 5 German Championship titles

Baubeginn Schloss Neuschwanstein
Building begins on Neuschwanstein Castle

'70

Schickt Armee in den siegreichen Deutsch-Französischen Krieg. Bayern wird Teil des neuen Deutschen Reiches unter dem 1. Deutschen Kaiser Wilhelm I.
Sends army to victory in the Franco-German War. Bavaria becomes part of the new German Reich under the first German Emperor, Wilhelm I.

'72

Europameister und Europas Fußballer des Jahres
UEFA European Championship and European Footballer of the Year

'74

Weltmeister
FIFA World Cup
1. von 3 Europapokalen der Landesmeister
1st of 3 UEFA Champions League Cups

Baubeginn Schloss Linderhof
Building begins on Linderhof Palace

'76

Weltpokalsieger
Intercontinental Cup

Letzter öffentlicher Auftritt vor der Generalprobe der Bayreuther Festspiele
Last public appearance at a dress rehearsal for the Bayreuth Festival

Ärger mit der Steuer: zahlt 1,8 Mio. DM (ca. 920.000 €) nach
Tax trouble: has to pay 1.8 mil. DM (ca. € 920,000) in back taxes

Umzug nach New York, Spieler bei Cosmos
Moves to New York, plays for the Cosmos

`77

`78

Baubeginn Schloss Herrenchiemsee
Building begins on Herrenchiemsee Palace

Rückkehr nach Deutschland, Spieler beim HSV
Returns to Germany, plays for HSV in Hamburg

`80

Karriereende in Deutschland
Ends career as player in Germany

`82

Kurze Rückkehr zu New York Cosmos, endgültiges Karriereende
Briefly returns to the New York Cosmos, final end of career as player

`83

Teamchef der Deutschen Nationalmannschaft
Team coach of German National Football Team

`84

Vize-Weltmeister als Teamchef
Team is runner-up in FIFA World Cup

`86

Wird durch Regierung entmündigt und nach Schloss Berg am Starnberger See gebracht. Ertrinkt am 13. Juni im See unter mysteriösen Umständen.
Deposed by the government and brought to Berg Castle on Lake Starnberg. Drowns in the lake on 13 June under mysterious circumstances.

Seither als *Kini* königliche Lichtgestalt
Since then remembered as *Kini*, *"Our Cherished King"*.

'90

Weltmeister als Teamchef: Beckenbauer wird zur Lichtgestalt
World champion as team chief: Beckenbauer becomes a leading light

Sybille Weimar (ehemalige DFB-Sekretärin former German Football Association secretary)

'91

Technischer Direktor bei Olympique Marseille; französischer Meister
Technical director of Olympique Marseille; French champion

Vizepräsident beim FCB, später Präsident und Ehrenpräsident
Vice-president of FC Bayern München, later president, then honorary president

2000

Joel Maximilian mit / with **Heidi Burmester (FC-Bayern-München-Sekretärin** / secretary**)**

2003

Francesca mit / with **Heidi**

2004

Scheidung von Sybille
Divorce from Sybille

2006

WM-Botschafter für die deutsche Bewerbung um die Austragung des Turniers 2006.
World Cup ambassador for Germany's bid to host the tournament in 2006.

Heidi Burmester

Bis heute kaiserliche Lichtgestalt
Still today an imperial shining light

Kaum jemand wird in Bayern so verehrt und verklärt wie Ludwig II. Einzig Fußballkaiser Franz Beckenbauer kommt an die Popularität des Märchenkönigs heran. Dabei könnten ihre Lebensläufe, die genau ein Jahrhundert trennen, nicht unterschiedlicher sein. Ein aristokratischer Vergleich. / King Ludwig II is venerated and glorified in Bavaria like hardly any other figure. Only the "emperor" of football, Franz Beckenbauer, comes close to matching the fairytale king's popularity. And yet the two men's biographies, separated by exactly one century, could hardly be more different. An aristocratic comparison.

Stern des Südens

Star of the South

Viel Feind', viel Ehr': Seit 50 Jahren dominiert der FC Bayern die Bundesliga. /
No guts, no glory: For 50 years FC Bayern has dominated the National League.

	1. Dekade / 1st decade **1965–1975**	**2. Dekade** / 2nd decade **1976–1985**	**3. Dekade** / 3rd decade **1986–1995**

PRÄGENDER KOPF DER EPOCHE KEY HEADS OF THE VARIOUS ERAS	**PAUL BREITNER** 1970–1974, 1978–1983	**KARL-HEINZ RUMMENIGGE** 1974–1984	**LOTHAR MATTHÄUS** 1984–1988, 1992–2000
Meisterschaften Championships	●●●●	●●●	●●●●●
DFB-Pokal DFB Cup	4 cups	2 cups	1 cup
Landesmeister Cup Champions League	2 trophies	1 trophy	
Stadien Stadiums	Grünwalder Stadion → Olympiastadion	Olympiastadion	Olympiastadion

4. Dekade / 4th decade
1996–2005

5. Dekade / 5th decade
seit / since 2006

OLIVER KAHN
1994–2008

PHILIPP LAHM
1995–2003, seit / since 2005

Anteilseigner der FC Bayern München AG
Shareholders in the FC Bayern München AG

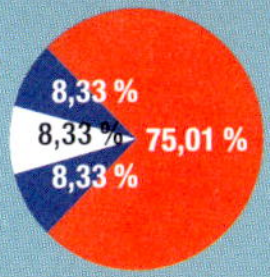

Allianz Arena

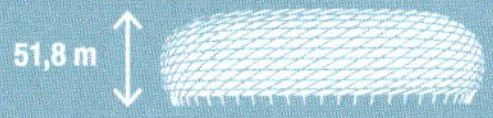

ca. 75.000
Zuschauer / spectators

Markenwert
Brand value

FCB-Spieler im deutschen WM-Kader
FCB players in the German World Cup squad

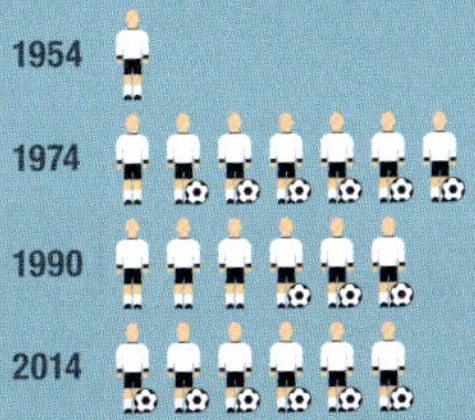

⚽ **im Finale dabei** / played in the finale

Unter Brüdern
Between brothers

Adidas und Puma gehören heute hinter Nike zu den größten internationalen Sportartikelherstellern. Sie sind erbitterte Konkurrenten auf dem Weltmarkt – dabei entstammen beide Konzerne einem Familienunternehmen aus der fränkischen Kleinstadt Herzogenaurach. / Today, Adidas and Puma are amongst the biggest international sportswear makers, second only to Nike. The two corporate groups are bitter rivals on the world market – and yet both stem from the same family-run business in the small Franconian town of Herzogenaurach.

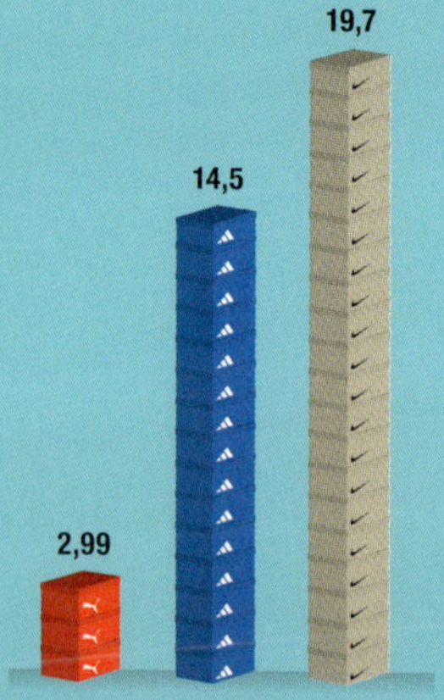

Umsatz / Turnover **2013 in Mrd. / bn €**

Mitarbeiter / Employees **2013**

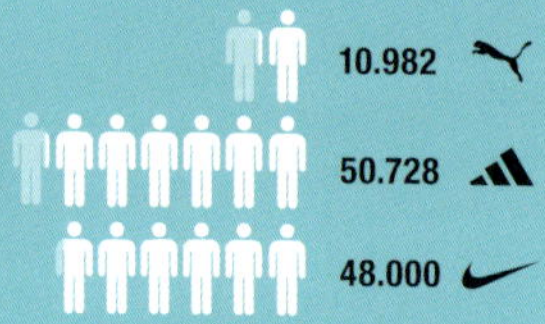

Rudolfs Familie zieht aus dem gemeinsamen Haus aus.
Rudolf's family moves out of the shared homestead.

2. Weltkrieg: Rudolf wird eingezogen.
World War II: Rudolf is drafted.

Frauen verstehen sich nicht, Familien entfremden sich.
The wives don't get along and the families become estranged.

Nachkommen verkaufen Ihre Adidas-Anteile
Descendants sell their Adidas shares.
1990
1989
Nachkommen verkaufen ihre Puma-Anteile
Descendants sell their Puma shares.
1978
Adi
1974
Rudolf
Firma wird aufgeteilt.
The company splits up.
Adidas (Kurzform von / short for Adi Dassler)
PUMA
adidas
Adi leitet zuhause das Unternehmen.
Adi runs the company back home.
1949
Adolf Dassler adidas Sportschuhe
1948
Puma Schuhfabrik
1943
NSDAP
Dassler-Brüder, beide in der NSDAP, profitieren von Hitlers Nachfrage.
Both Dassler brothers are in the Nazi Party and profit from the high demand under Hitler.
1934
Adi
Käthe
Rudolf
Friedl
1928
Erste Dassler-Schuhe bei Olympia in Amsterdam
First Dassler shoes at the Olympics, in Amsterdam
1924
Christoph & Paulina Dassler, Herzogenaurach
Dassler
Söhne Adolf und Rudolf gründen „Gebrüder Dassler Schuhfabrik“
Sons Adolf and Rudolf found the “Dassler Brothers Shoe Factory”.

Wer hat's erfunden?
Who invented it?

Mehr als ein Viertel aller deutschen Patente werden im Freistaat angemeldet. Aber bereits vor Siemens und Co. veränderten Innovationen aus Bayern die Welt. / More than a quarter of all German patents originate in Bavaria. But even before Siemer and the rest came onto the scene, Bavarian innovations were changing the world.

um / around **1504**

Taschenuhr
Pocket watch
Peter Henlein
(Nürnberg)

MP3-Format
MP3 format
Karlheinz Brandenburg
(Erlangen)

1982

VON BAYERN GEMACHTE ERFINDUNGEN
INVENTIONS MADE BY BAVARIANS

1655

Rollstuhl
Wheelchair
Stephan Farfler
(Altdorf bei / near **Nürnberg)**

1815

Metronom
Metronome
Johann Nepomuk Mälzel
(Regensburg)

1872

Jeans
Levi Strauss
(Buttenheim)

Mitte 19. Jh.
Mid-19th century

Kneipp-Medizin und Wasserkur mit Wassertreten
Kneipp medicine and hydrotherapy, including treading water
Sebastian Anton Kneipp
(Stephansried)

1907

„Mensch ärgere Dich nicht"
A game similar to Ludo
Josef Friedrich Schmidt
(München / Munich**)**

1929

Tempo-Taschentuch
Tempo paper handkerchief
Vereinigte Papierwerke
Nürnberg

1951

Airbag
Walter Linderer
(München / Munich**)**

1952

Skibindung
Ski bindings
Hannes Marker
(Garmisch-Partenkirchen)

1972

Bobby-Car
Bobby-Car

Die Herren der Ringe
The Lords of the Rings

Audi-Modelle werden weltweit verkauft – und längst auch weltweit produziert. Geschichte einer bayerischen Globalisierung / Audi models are sold worldwide – and have long been produced worldwide as well. The story of a Bavarian globalisation.

AUTOMOBILPRODUKTION IM IN- UND AUSLAND (INKL. LAMBORGHINI)
AUTOMOBILE PRODUCTION IN GERMANY AND ABROAD (INCL. LAMBORGHINI)

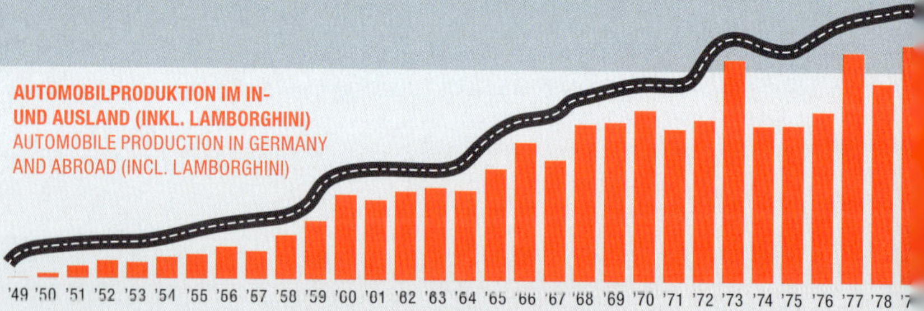

	gesamt total
'49	504
'50	8.253
'51	22.393
'52	32.593
'53	29.762
'54	39.419
'55	45.061
'56	59.142
'57	51.074
'58	80.983
'59	107.388
'60	156.268
'61	146.867
'62	163.286
'63	170.287
'64	165.542
'65	205.910
'66	254.802
'67	222.672
'68	289.577
'69	293.673
'70	316.539
'71	282.200
'72	299.484
'73	409.793
'74	288.556
'75	289.561
'76	314.729
'77	424.171
'78	368.042
'7	[illegible]

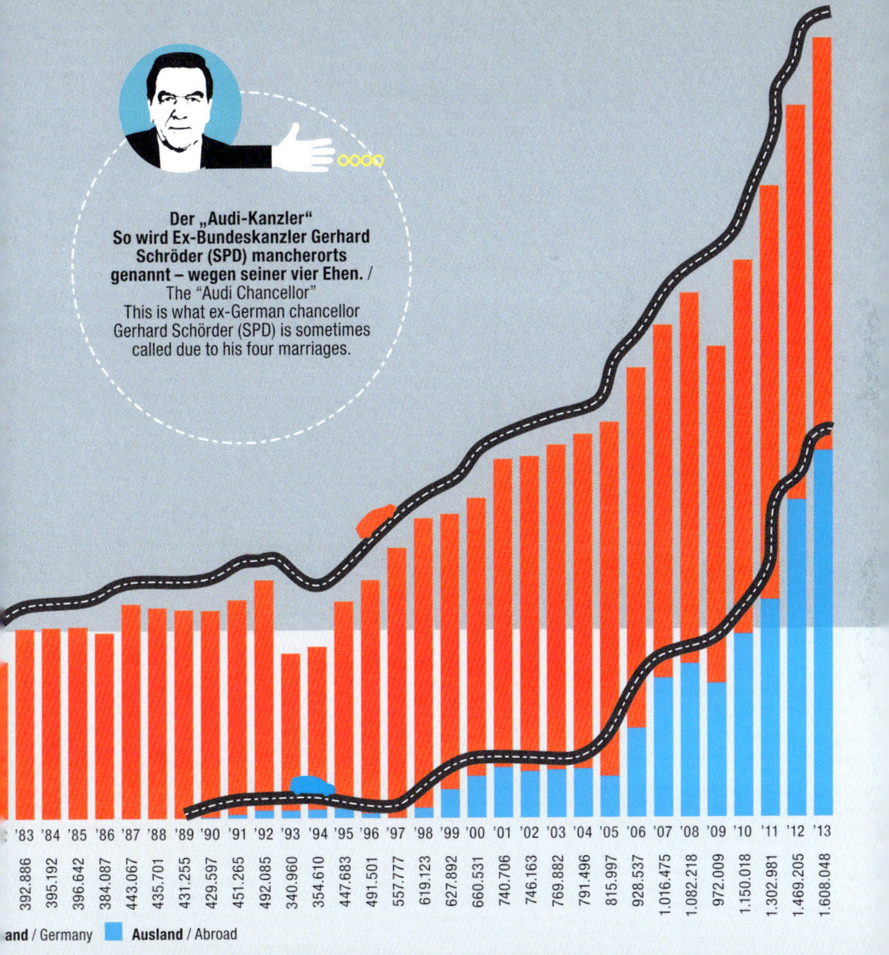
Der „Audi-Kanzler“
So wird Ex-Bundeskanzler Gerhard Schröder (SPD) mancherorts genannt – wegen seiner vier Ehen. /
The “Audi Chancellor”
This is what ex-German chancellor Gerhard Schörder (SPD) is sometimes called due to his four marriages.
'83 '84 '85 '86 '87 '88 '89 '90 '91 '92 '93 '94 '95 '96 '97 '98 '99 '00 '01 '02 '03 '04 '05 '06 '07 '08 '09 '10 '11 '12 '13
392.886
395.192
396.642
384.087
443.067
435.701
431.255
429.597
451.265
492.085
340.960
354.610
447.683
491.501
557.777
619.123
627.892
660.531
740.706
746.163
769.882
791.496
815.997
928.537
1.016.475
1.082.218
972.009
1.150.018
1.302.981
1.469.205
1.608.048
and / Germany
Ausland / Abroad

Heißer Kühler
Radiant radiators

Mitarbeiter Employees

Autoproduktion Automobile production

BMW baut weltberühmte Autos mit einem einzigartigen Design – insbesondere weger der „Doppel-Niere". Eine frontale Geschichte / BMW makes world-famous cars with exceptional design features – especially the unique "double kidney" grille. An up-front history

1916

7.3.1916 Gründung der Bayerischen Motoren Werke AG. Founding of the Bayerische Motoren Werke AG.

1918 — 800 (Mitarbeiter)

Ausschließlich Produktion von Flugmotoren. Production of aircraft engines only

1920 er-Jahre / s

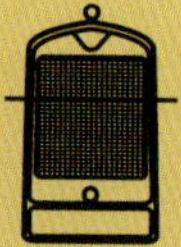

1929 BMW 3/15 — Mitarbeiter: 3.309 — Autoproduktion: 7.873

1930 er-Jahre / s

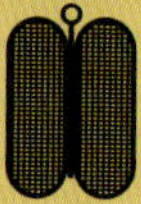

1933 BMW 303 — Mitarbeiter: 6.514 — Autoproduktion: 5.839

1940 er-Jahre / s

Bis / Until 1941 BMW 326 — Mitarbeiter: 40.175

Zwangsarbeit bei BMW: Herstellung von Flugmotoren fü die Luftwaffe, Autoproduktion b 1952 eingestellt / Forced labour BMW: production of aircraft engin for the Luftwaffe, automobile production suspended until 1952

1950 er-Jahre / s

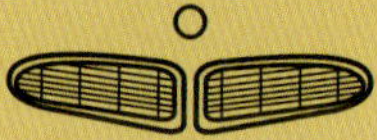

1956 Roadster BMW 507 — Mitarbeiter: 5.757 — Autoproduktion: 35.483

1960 er-Jahre
s

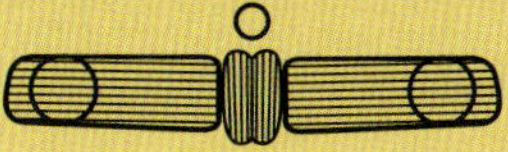

1962
BMW 1500

9.189

53.527

1970 er-Jahre
s

1975
3er BMW E21

28.989

221.298

1980 er-Jahre
s

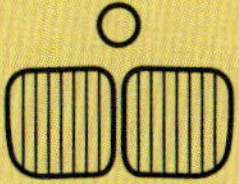

1987
5er BMW E34

54.861

461.340

1990 er-Jahre
s

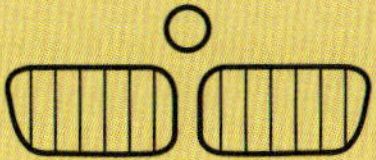

1994
7er BMW E38

109.362

948.683
(inkl. / incl.
Rover Group)

2000 Die
Nuller-Jahre
s

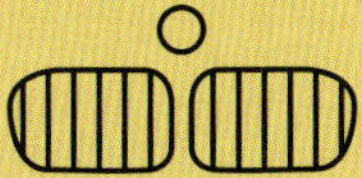

2006
SUV BMW
X5 E70

106.575

1.366.838
(inkl. / incl.
MINI, Rolls-Royce)

2010 er-Jahre
s

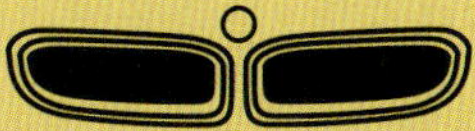

2013
Hybrid i8

110.351

2.006.366
(inkl. / incl.
MINI, Rolls-Royce)

Ein Geben und Nehmen
Give and take

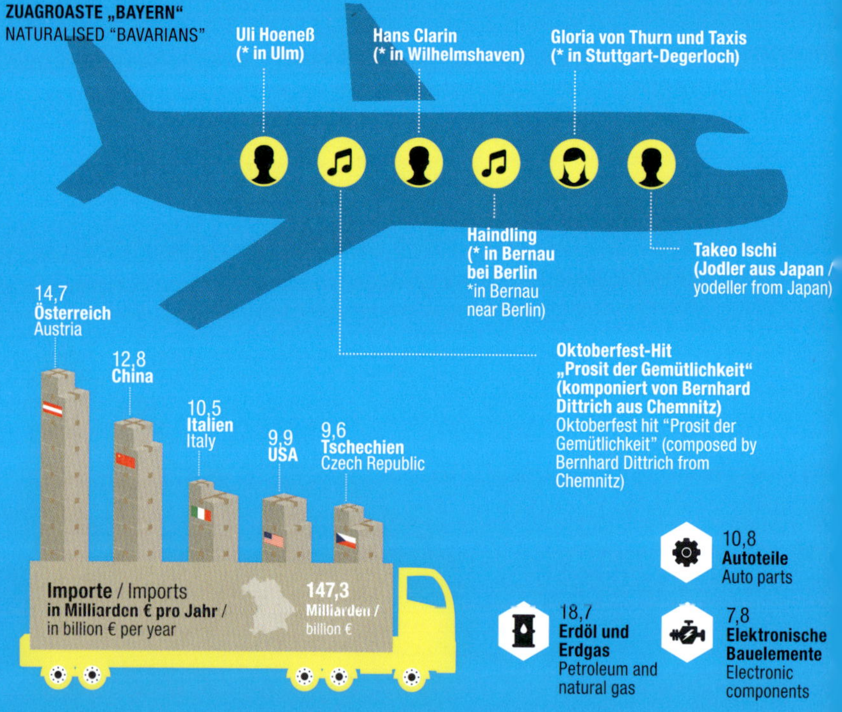

Das alte Rein-Raus-Spiel: Die wichtigsten Importe und Exporte des Freistaats / In again, out again: Bavaria's prime imports and exports

OUTGESOURCTE BAYERN
OUTSOURCED BAVARIANS

Henry Kissinger (* in Fürth, später US-Außenminister / b. in Fürth, later US Secretary of State)

Oliver Kahn (Juror in chinesischer Casting-Sendung / juror in a Chinese casting show)

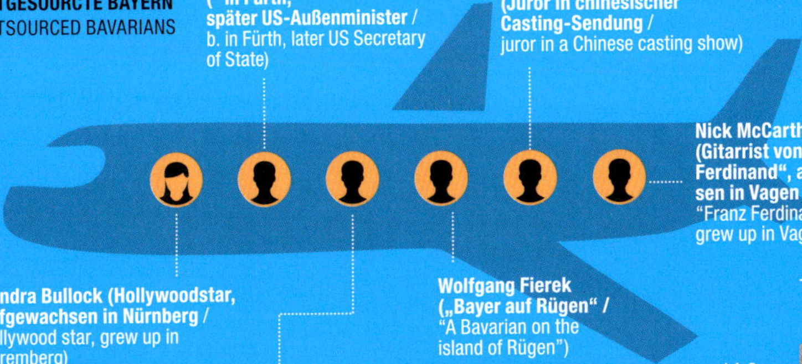

Nick McCarthy (Gitarrist von „Franz Ferdinand", aufgewachsen in Vagen / "Franz Ferdinand" guitarist, grew up in Vagen)

Sandra Bullock (Hollywoodstar, aufgewachsen in Nürnberg / Hollywood star, grew up in Nuremberg)

Wolfgang Fierek („Bayer auf Rügen" / "A Bavarian on the island of Rügen")

Christian Karl Gerhartsreiter (Hochstapler aus Siegsdorf, in den USA als der „Falsche Rockefeller" bekannt / Con man from Siegsdorf, known in the USA as a Rockefeller imposter)

12,1
Autoteile
Auto parts

32,3
Autos
Automobiles

9,6
Geräte zur Elektrizitätserzeugung und -verteilung
Devices for generating and distributing electricity

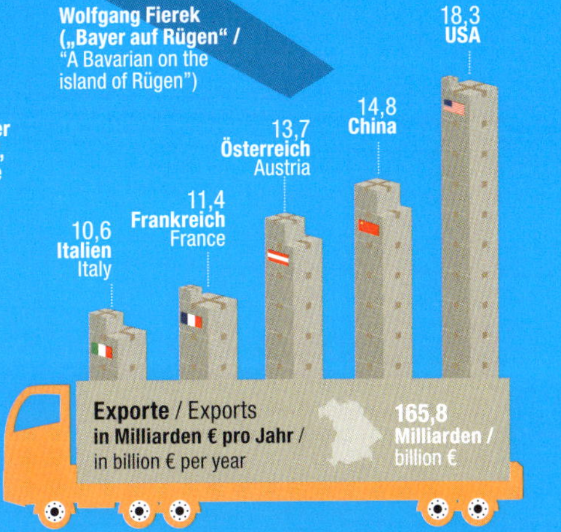

Über den Wolken
Up above the clouds

Der Verkehr am weiß-blauen Himmel /
Air traffic in the white-and-blue sky

NUE **Flughafen Nürnberg**
Nuremberg Airport

61.257
Flüge pro Jahr
flights per year

START
1955
Eröffnung
Year opened

870
Beschäftigte
employees

3,262 Mio. / mil.
Passagiere pro Jahr passengers per year

1
Start- und Landebahn
runway

519 ha
Fläche / Area

Bester Deutscher Flughafen
(Business Traveller Award 2014)
Best German Airport
(Business Traveller Award 2014)

FMM **Flughafen Memmingen-Allgäu /**
Memmingen-Allgäu Airport

14.929
Flüge pro Jahr
flights per year

START
1936
Eröffnung
Year opened

2004
Wiedereröffnung
Reopened

98
Beschäftigte
employees

750.315
Passagiere pro Jahr passengers per year

1
Start- und Landebahn
runway

145 ha
Fläche / Area

629 m
Höchstgelegener Verkehrsflughafen Deutschlands
Highest altitude of any commercial airport in Germany

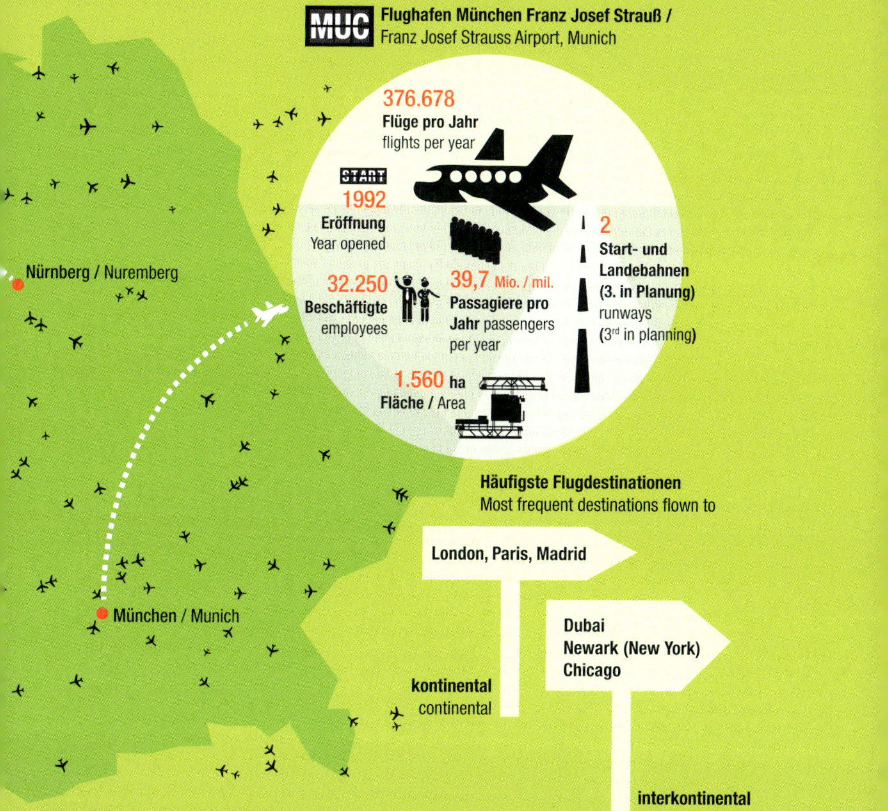

11:41 **Momentaufnahme des Luftraums über dem Freistaat an einem beliebigen Dienstag um 11:41 Uhr**

Snapshop of the airspace over Bavaria at 11:41 am on a typical Tuesday

Und wer zahlt's? Mia!
And who has to pay? We do!

Was in Bayern wie viel kostet / The cost of living in Bavaria

19,50 €

Fingerhaklschlaufe
Loop used in Fingerhakeln gan

1 €

Eintritt Pinakotheken (München), sonntags
Admission to the Pinakothek Museums (Munich) on Sunday

1,49 €

Obatzda bei Aldi Süd
Obatzda cheese at Aldi Süd

550 €

Maßgeschneiderte Hirschlederh
Bespoke deer-leather trousers

10,50 €

Schweinsbraten mit Knödl und Salat im Biergarten am Viktualienmarkt
Pork roast with dumplings and salad at the Viktualienmarkt beer garden

2 Paar Weißwürste beim Käfer
2 pairs of white sausages at Käfer
6,30 €

1.400.000 €
Tatort-Folge aus München
Munich-based episode of the Tatort TV series

55.000.000 €

Marktwert von Thomas Müller (FC Baye
Market value of Thomas Müller (FC Bayern

19.000.000 €
Marktwert aller 34 Spieler des FC Ingolstadt
Market value of all 34 FC Ingolstadt team members

Alphorn 1.600 €
Alphorn

Süddeutsche Zeitun
Süddeutsche Zeitung
ab/from 2,50 €

„Mang-Nase“ Schönheitsoperation in der Bodenseeklinik
“Mang nose” cosmetic surgery at the famous clinic on the Lake of Constance
ab/from 4.000 €

4 € **Eintritt in die Walhalla (Regensburg)**
Admission to Walhalla (Regensburg)

Brezn bei Müller Höflinger
Pretzel at Müller Höflinger
0,58 €

Skipass Oberstdorf Fellhorn-Kanzelwand, 1 Tag, Erwachsene Ski pass for Oberstdorf Fellhorn-Kanzelwand, 1 day, adult
35,50 €

2,49 €
Playmobil-Figur
Playmobil figure

3 €

ab/from 31,99 €
Bobby-Car

ab/from 99 €
Flug München–Berlin–München, Lufthansa
Flight Munich–Berlin–Munich, Lufthansa

Tasse Glühwein auf dem Nürnberger Christkindlesmarkt
Mug of mulled wine at the Nuremberg Christkindlesmarkt

18 €
Eintritt zur Spielwarenmesse in Nürnberg, Erwachsene (Kinder unter 16 Jahren haben keinen Zutritt.)
Admission to the Nuremberg Toy Fair, adult (Children under 16 are not admitted.)

4,40 €
Kaffee Dallmayr Prodomo, 250 g
Dallmayr Prodomo coffee 250 g

0 €
Studiengebühren
University tuition fees

5 €
Fahrt mit dem Oktoberfest-Riesenrad
A ride on the Oktoberfest Ferris wheel

23 +5 +5 +5 +5 €

yernticket (Die 1. Person zahlt 23 €, bis zu 4 weitere Mitfahrer je 5 €.)
yernticket for public transport (The 1st person pays € 23 and up to 4 fellow-passengers pay € 5 each.)

Flotter Dreier
Threesomes

Was verbirgt sich hinter den drei Begriffen? Der Bayern-Test für ehrgeizige Zuagroaste und heimische Gscheidhaferl / What might each set of three terms have in common? The Bavaria test for ambitious newcomers and native know-it-alls

1 + 2 + 3 = 1

 Audi +  ERC +  Frankenstein = 2

 Flo +  Peter +  Rüde = 3

 Batic +  Leitmayr +  5er BMW = 4

 **Weißwein** White wine +  **Zitronenlimo** Lemonade +  **Kirschlikör** Cherry liqueur = 5

 **Kaiserdom** Imperial Cathedral +  **Altstadt** Historic centre +  **Brose Baskets** = 6

maß (Laterenmass cocktail), **6** Bamberg, **7** Strauss, **8** Musikantenstadl (Stars of Musikantenstadl folk music TV show), **9** Neureuther,

anz-Josef + Richard + Levi = 7

tefan Mross + Florian Silbereisen + Margot & Maria Hellwig = 8

osi + Christian + Felix = 9

ans + Sophie + Mehmet = 10

Vasser / Vater + Malz / Malt + Hopfen / Hops = 11

INA + FAG + LUK = 12

ittelalter / iddle Ages + Amerikaner / Americans + Japaner / Japanese = 13

ans + Stofferl + Michael = 14

Lösungen / Solutions: **1** Gsuffa! (Bottoms up!), **2** Ingolstadt, **3** Sportfreunde Stiller, **4** Tatort aus München (Tatort TV crime show fro
10 Scholl, **11** Reinheitsgebot (Germany purity law for beer) **12** Schaeffler, **13** Rothenburg ob der Tauber, **14** Biermösl Blosn

Lang lang

It's a long, long road

Und jetzt alle: Strecken! / And now everyone: stretch!

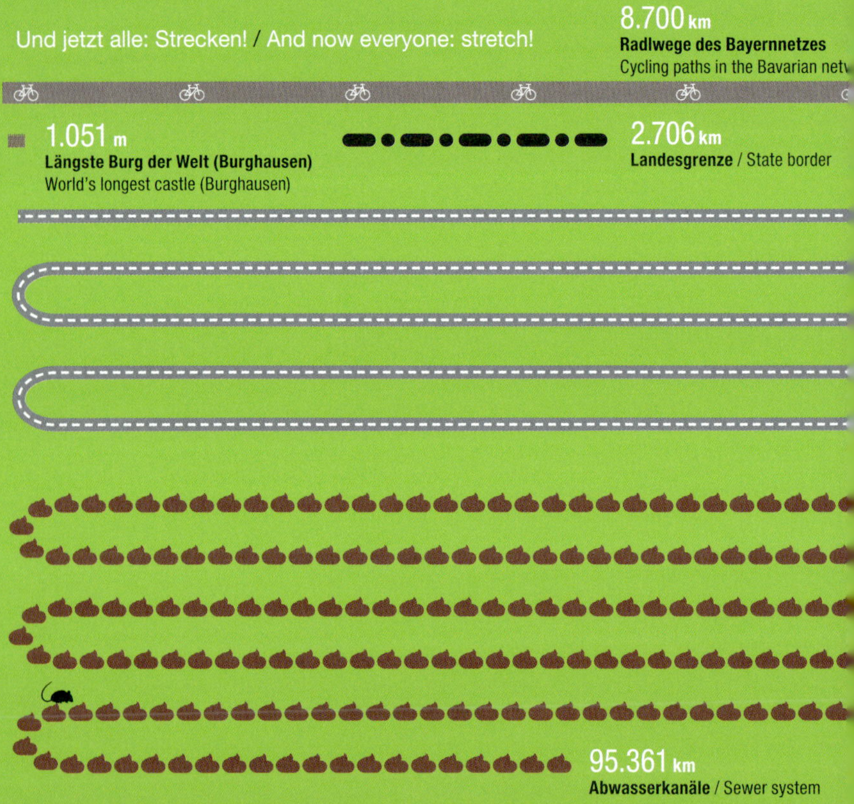

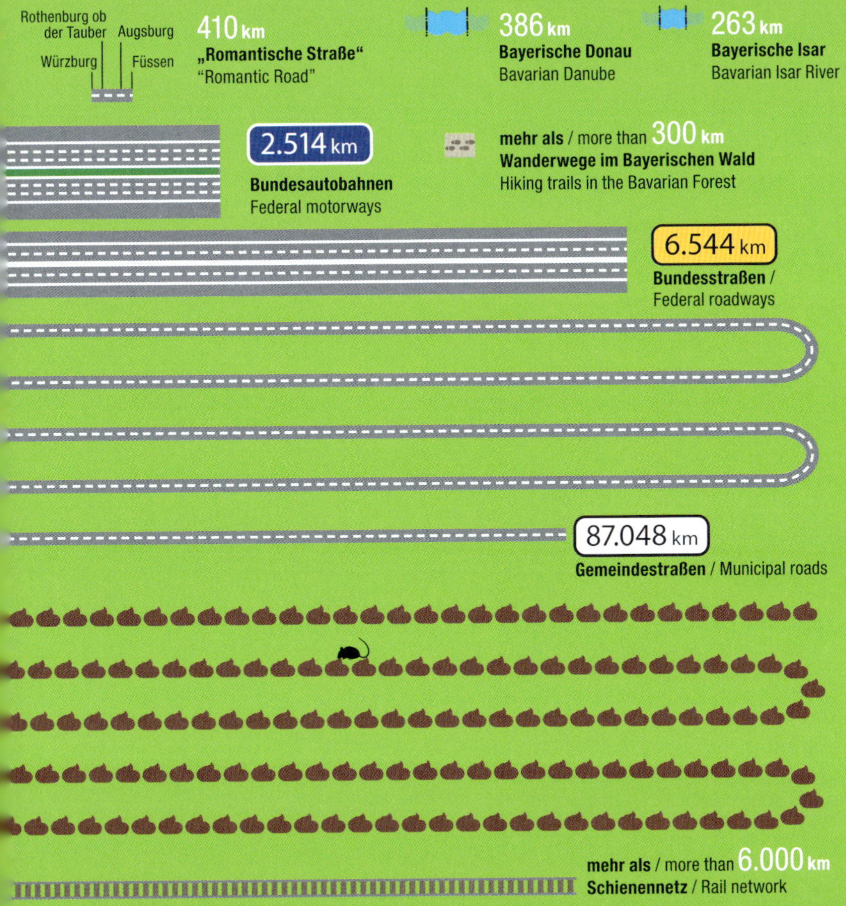

Rothenburg ob der Tauber
Augsburg
Würzburg
Füssen
410 km
„Romantische Straße“
“Romantic Road”
386 km
Bayerische Donau
Bavarian Danube
263 km
Bayerische Isar
Bavarian Isar River
2.514 km
Bundesautobahnen
Federal motorways
mehr als / more than 300 km
Wanderwege im Bayerischen Wald
Hiking trails in the Bavarian Forest
6.544 km
Bundesstraßen /
Federal roadways
87.048 km
Gemeindestraßen / Municipal roads
mehr als / more than 6.000 km
Schienennetz / Rail network

Kopf an Kopf
Head to head

Leicht zu erkennen, oft schwer zu verstehen: Bayerns Repräsentanten / Easy to recognise, often hard to understand: Bavarian figureheads

Doris Dörrie

Thomas Gottschalk

Benedikt XVI.
(Joseph Aloisius Ratzinger)

Karl Valentin
(Valentin Ludwig Fey

Erni Singerl

Rudolph Moshammer

Ludwig II.

Christian Ude

Gloria von Thurn
und Taxis

Dirk Nowitzki

Uschi Obermaier

Charlotte Knobloch

Ilse Aigner

Uli Hoeneß

Claus von Stauffenberg

Günther Kaufmann

oe Kaeser (Josef Käser)

Barbara Schöneberger

Lion Feuchtwanger

Gisela Schneeberger

Martina Gedeck

Gerhard Polt

Peter Gauweiler

Franz-Josef Strauß

Christine Neubauer

Franz-Xaver Kroetz

Helmut Dietl

Erwin Pelzig

So soll es sein
What shall be, shall be

Prognosen für den Freistaat, oder wie Karl Valentin schon sagte: „Die Zukunft war früher auch besser.“ / Forecasts for Bavaria or, as Karl Valentin once said: “The future just isn’t what it used to be.”

34 %

Anteil der über 60-Jährigen im Jahr 2029
Ratio of persons over 60 in 2029

+1,5 %
pro Jahr / per year

Wirtschaftswachstum bis 2040
Economic growth by 2040

46,4
Jahre / years

Durchschnittsalter 2029
Average age in 2029

79,7
Jahre / years

84,4
Jahre / years

Lebenserwartung 2029
Life expectancy by 2029

30 %

Angestrebter Anteil erneuerbarer Energien an der Stromerzeugung 2020
Targeted ratio of renewable energies used for electricity generation by 2020

Atomausstieg abgeschlossen bis 2022 (nach Stilllegung des Atommeilers Isar II)
Nuclear phase-out completed by 2022 (after shutdown of Isar II nuclear power station)

Bevölkerungsentwicklung in den kreisfreien Städten und Landkreisen Bayerns
Population development in Bavaria's counties and independent cities
Veränderung 2032 gegenüber 2012
Changes between 2012 and 2032

Das letzte Stück
The last piece

Sie wissen immer noch nicht total alles über Bayern? Vielleicht beantwortet dieses Torten-Pichelsteiner die letzten offenen Fragen. / You still don't know everything there is to know about Bavaria? Perhaps this Pichelsteiner stew of pie charts will answer your last remaining questions.

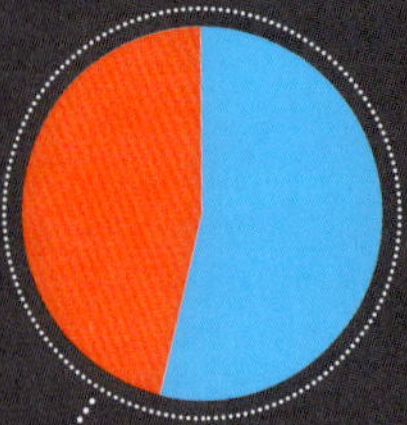

Umfrage im Freistaat: Fühlen Sie sich eher als Bayer oder als Deutscher?
Survey taken in Bavaria: Do you feel more like a Bavarian or a German?

- **54 % Bayer** / Bavarian
- **46 % Deutscher** / German

Mitglieder des Ostbayerischen Bart- und Schnauzerclubs
Members of the East Bavaria Beard and Moustache Club

- **77,5 % männlich** / male
- **22,5 % weiblich** / female

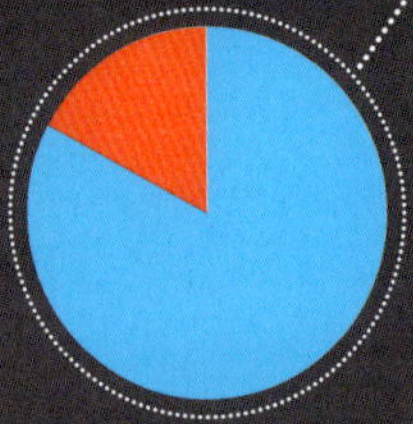

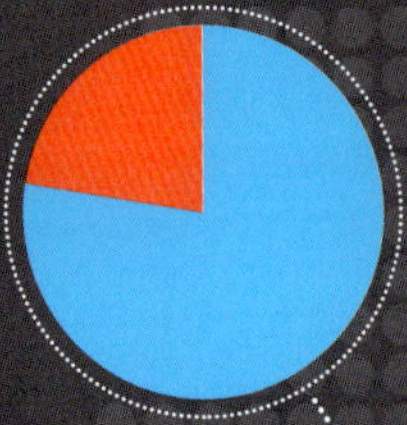

„Mariä Himmelfahrt"
Feast of the Assumption (15.8.)

- **82,9 % gesetzlicher Feiertag in 1.704 von insgesamt 2.056 Gemeinden**
bank holiday in 1,704 of the total 2,056 municipalities

Ergebnisse der letzten Landtagswahl (2013)
Results of the last parliamentary elections (2013)

- **47,7 % CSU** / Christian Social Union
- **20,6 % SPD** / Social Democratic Party
- **9,0 % Freie Wähler** / Free Voters
- **8,6 % Grüne** / The Greens
- **3,3 % FDP** / Free Democratic Party
- **2,1 % Linke** / The Left
- **2,1 % Bayernpartei** / Bavaria Party
- **2,0 % ÖDP** / Ecological Democratic Party
- **4,6 % Sonstige** / Others

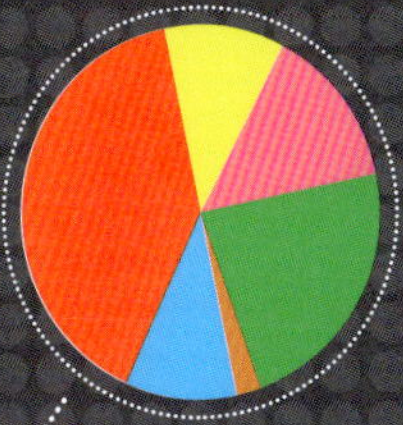

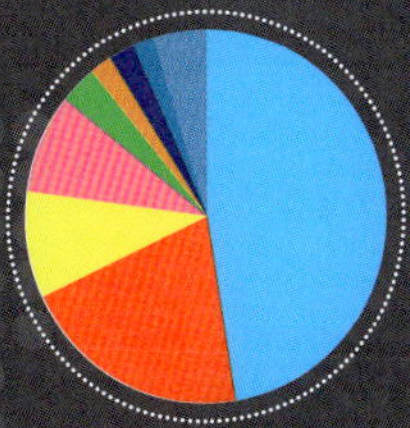

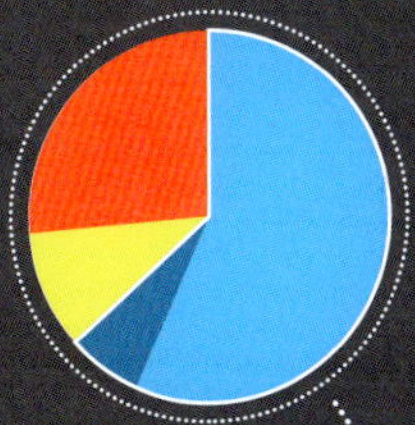

Zutaten Leberkäs / Leberkäs ingredients

- **10 % Rindfleisch** / beef
- **40 % Schweinefleisch** / pork
- **11 % Schweinebacken** / pork cheek
- **14 % Speck** / bacon
- **23 % Eis und Wasser** / ice and water
- **2 % Nitritpökelsalz** / nitrite curing salt

Uferlänge des Bodensees
Lake Constance shoreline

- **173 km in Deutschland** / Germany
  davon / thereof
  - **155 km in Baden-Württemberg**
  - **18 km in Bayern** / Bavaria
- **28 km in Österreich** / Austria
- **72 km in der Schweiz** / Switzerland

Quellen / References

11FREUNDE Verlag GmbH & Co.KG, www.11freunde.de

Abendzeitung München, www.abendzeitung-muenchen.de

Ärzte Zeitung online, www.aerztezeitung.de

Allgäu Airport – Flughafen Memmingen, www.allgaeu-airport.de

Allianz Arena München Stadion GmbH, www.allianz-arena.de

Alois Dallmayr KG, www.dallmayr-versand.de

Alphornbau Alois Biermaier, Bischofswiesen, www.alphornbau-biermaier.de

Antenne Bayern GmbH & Co. KG, www.antenne.de

Arte G.E.I.E., www.arte.tv

Audi AG, www.audi.de

Audi AG, Audi MediaServices, www.audimediaservices.com

Augsburger Allgemeine Zeitung, www.augsburger-allgemeine.de

Aventura do Brasil Viagens Ltda. ME, www.aventuradobrasil.de

Baumann, Franziska: Wandern am Wasser Bayerische Alpen: Bergseen, Schluchten und Wildbäche. Oberhaching: Rother 2013

Bayerische Landesärztekammer, www.blaek.de

Bayerische Landesanstalt für Landwirtschaft, www.lfl.bayern.de

Bayerische Landesanstalt für Wald und Forstwirtschaft, www.lwf.bayern.de

Bayerische Motoren Werke AG, BMW Welt, www.bmw-welt.com

Bayerische Seenschifffahrt GmbH, www.seenschifffahrt.de

Bayerische Staatszeitung, www.bayerische-staatszeitung.de

Bayerische Vermessungsverwaltung, http://vermessung.bayern.de

Bayerische Verwaltung der staatlichen Schlösser, Gärten und Seen, www.schloesser.bayern.de

Bayerischer Brauereibund e. V., www.bayrisch-bier.de

Bayerischer Jagdverband e. V., www.jagd-bayern.de

Bayerischer Rundfunk, www.br.de

Bayerisches Landesamt für Statistik und Datenverarbeitung, Statistisches Jahrbuch für Bayern 2013

Bayerisches Landesamt für Statistik und Datenverarbeitung, www.statistik.bayern.de

Bayerisches Landesamt für Umwelt, www.lfu.bayern.de

Bayerisches Staatsministerium der Finanzen, für Landesentwicklung und Heimat, www.stmf.bayern.de

Bayerisches Staatsministerium des Innern, für Bau und Verkehr, www.stmi.bayern.de

Bayerisches Staatsministerium für Arbeit und Soziales, Familie und Integration, www.stmas.bayern.de

Bayerisches Staatsministerium für Ernährung, Landwirtschaft und Forsten, www.stmelf.bayern.de

Bayerisches Staatsministerium für Ernährung, Landwirtschaft und Forsten, Spezialitätendatenbank, www.spezialitaetenland-bayern.de

Bayerisches Staatsministerium für Gesundheit und Pflege, www.stmgp.bayern.de

Bayerisches Staatsministerium für Umwelt und Verbraucherschutz, Gletscherbericht, www.stmuv.bayern.de

BAYERN TOURISMUS Marketing GmbH, www.bayern.by

Bayreuther Festspiele GmbH, www.bayreuther-festspiele.de

bergfex GmbH, www.bergfex.de

Bergsteiger, www.bergsteiger.de

Bergwacht Bayern, www.bergwacht-bayern.de

Bernstein, Martin (Hrsg.): Berge, Schlösser, Königsträume – Auf den Spuren König Ludwigs II. Süddeutsche Zeitung Edition 2011

Bielefeld, Knud, www.beliebte-vornamen.de

Biermann, Christoph / Köster, Philipp: Fast alles über 50 Jahre Bundesliga. Köln: Kiepenheuer & Witsch 2013

BMW Group, www.bmwgroup.com

BÖLW, Bund Ökologische Lebensmittelwirtschaft e. V., www.boelw.de

Bootsverleih Stöffl, Prien am Chiemsee, www.stoeffl.de

Burghauser Touristik GmbH, http://tourismus.burghausen.de

Council on Tall Buildings and Urban Habitat, The Skyscraper Center, http://skyscrapercenter.com

Curd Biedermann Biketouristik, www.bayernbike.de

DAK-Gesundheit, www.dak.de

Deutsche Bahn AG, www.bahn.com

Deutscher Alpenverein, www.alpenverein.de

Donaukurier Ingolstadt, www.donaukurier.de

dpa, Deutsche Presse-Agentur GmbH, www.dpa.de

Draxler, Alfred / Beckenbauer, Franz: 40 Jahre Bundesliga. Berlin: Ullstein 2003

Eigene Recherche / The authors' own research

Energie-Atlas Bayern, www.energieatlas.bayern.de

FC Bayern München AG, www.fcbayern.de

Feinkost Käfer, München, http://shop.feinkost-kaefer.de

Flightradar24, www.flightradar24.com

Flughafen München „Franz Josef Strauß", www.munich-airport.de

Flughafen Nürnberg, www.airport-nuernberg.de

Focus Magazin Verlag GmbH, www.focus.de

Frankfurter Allgemeine Zeitung GmbH, www.faz.de

Füssen Tourismus und Marketing, www.fuessen.de

Gesellschaft für Nachrichten und Zeitgeschehen mbH, www.n24.de

Google Maps, https://maps.google.com

Gruber, Thomas: Ansichtssache Bayern: Annäherungen an eine Heimat, Frankfurter Societäts-Druckerei 2010

Handelsblatt GmbH, www.handelsblatt.com

Haus der Bayerischen Geschichte, München, www.hdbg.de

Herold, Frank, www.marketing-blog.biz

Hochschule für angewandte Wissenschaften – Hochschule Ansbach, www.jupo-bayern.de

mmowelt AG, ttp://presse.immowelt.de

NSM-Initiative Neue Soziale Marktwirtschaft GmbH, www.bundeslaenderranking.de

Kirchinger, Johann: Der nicht ontrollierbare Raum. Die Deutung er bäuerlichen Arbeitswelt in er Moderne – im Spiegel der Eigennamen für Nutztiere. In: Beiträge zur Namenforschung 50 (2014)

Klausmann, Hubert: Atlas der Familiennamen von Bayern. Ostfildern: Thorbecke 2009

Konradin Medien GmbH, www.wissen.de

Lederhosen Stangassinger, Berchtesgaden, www.lederhosenmacher.com

Meintz, René, www.kirchenaustritt.de

Metzgerei Magnus Bauch, München, http://mbwassonst.de

München Betriebs-GmbH & Co. KG, www.muenchen.de

Münchner Merkur, www.merkur-online.de

Münchner Wochenanzeiger, www.wochenanzeiger-muenchen.de

Nationalpark Bayerischer Wald, www.nationalpark-bayerischer-wald.de

Neue Presse Multimedia GmbH, www.heimatzeitung.de

Neumann, Jürgen / Prokopetz, Johannes. Bayerns lustigste Ortsnamen. Frankfurt/Main: Societätsverlag 2010

Nike Annual Report, http://investors.nikeinc.com

Ostbayerischer Bart- und Schnauzerclub 1996 e. V., www.bcostbayern.de

Playboy Deutschland Publishing GmbH, www.playboy.de

Polt, Gerhard: Album „Die Klassiker"

Proplanta GmbH & Co. KG, www.proplanta.de

Puma Annual Report, www.puma-annual-report.com

Renn, Manfred / König, Werner: Kleiner Bayerischer Sprachatlas. München: dtv 2009

Robert-Koch-Institut, Abteilung für Epidemiologie und Gesundheitsberichterstattung (Hrsg.): Kleinräumige Bedarfsprognosen, 2011

RP Digital GmbH, www.rp-online.de

Sambaco GmbH, www.samba-festival.de

Siemens AG, www.siemens.com

Spiegel online GmbH, www.spiegel.de

Stadt Altötting, www.altoetting.de

Staffelsee-Gymnasium Murnau, Kulturpfad Ludwig II., http://ludwig.cmswp.de

Statista GmbH, http://de.statista.com

Statistisches Bundesamt, www.destatis.de

Stephan Straßer, Gehörlosenverband München und Umland e. V.

stern.de GmbH, www.stern.de

Stiftung Haus der Geschichte der Bundesrepublik Deutschland, www.hdg.de

Süddeutsche Zeitung, www.sueddeutsche.de

The Brand Finance Institute, www.brandfinance.com

Tourismus Oberstdorf, www.oberstdorf.de

Transfermarkt GmbH & Co. KG, www.transfermarkt.de

vbw, Vereinigung der Bayerischen Wirtschaft e. V., www.vbw-bayern.de

Wikipedia

WWF Deutschland, www.wwf.de

www.adidas-group.com

www.amazon.de

www.autobild.de

www.cinemaxx.de

www.gmu.de

www.kliniken.de

www.muenchen.de

www.nachrichten.at

www.nurfussball.com

www.oktoberfest.de

www.wm-trikots.org

www.youtube.com/watch?v=FW6P_crgp8M

Zur Aubinger Einkehr, www.aubinger-einkehr-muenchen.de

Wichtigste Datenquelle / Main data source: Bayerisches Landesamt für Statistik und Datenverarbeitung

Dank an / Thanks to: meine Familie / my family
sowie an / as well as to: Magnus Bauch, Annika Biss, Joachim Cordshagen, Barbara Ettl, Bernhard Greller, Barbara Kink, Dominik Prantl, Stephan Straßer, Irene Warres. Audi AG, Bayerischer Jagdverband e. V., BMW AG, Haus der Bayerischen Geschichte

Auch bei Folio erschienen / Also available from Folio:

Total alles über Südtirol / Alto Adige – Tutto di tutto / The Complete South Tyrol
Hermann Gummerer / Franziska Hack
Infographics: no.parking
ISBN 978-3-85256-607-8

Total alles über Österreich / The Complete Austria
Sonja¥Franzke
Infographics: no.parking
ISBN 978-3-85256-630-6

Total alles über Bayern / The Complete Bavaria
Martin Wittmann
Infographics: no.parking
ISBN 978-3-85256-646-7

Total alles über die Schweiz / The Complete Switzerland
Susann Sitzler
Infographics: no.parking
ISBN 978-3-85256-673-3

Pocket-Reihe / Pocket series:

Total alles über Südtirol / Alto Adige – Tutto di tutto / The Complete South Tyrol, Pocket edition
Hermann Gummerer / Franziska Hack
Infographics: no.parking
ISBN 978-3-85256-656-6

Total alles über Wien / The Complete Vienna, Pocket edition
Sonja Franzke
Infographics: no.parking
ISBN 978-3-85256-665-8

1. Auflage / edition 2015

Idee & Konzept / Idea & Concept: Hermann Gummerer, Franziska Maria Hack; no.parking
Translation into English: Jennifer Taylor
Lektorat / Proofreading: Franziska Maria Hack, Hermann Gummerer
Druckvorstufe / Prepress Service: Typoplus, Frangart
Grafik und Umbruch / Graphic design: no.parking, Vicenza
Printed in Europe
ISBN 978-3-85256-674-0

www.folioverlag.com